TOUGH SKIN

A Journey of Survival and Persevering Life's Challenges

OFTEN TIMES IN LIFE, THE STORM IS REQUIRED IN ORDER TO RECEIVE THE BLESSING

Samira L. Jones

with Lauren A. Ransome, Editor

Picture Perfect Page

L.A.E. Publishing Group

Printing

Set in 12-point Soft Touch by Gasch Printing Services

Jones, Samira L.

Tough Skin: A Journey of Survival and Persevering Life's
Challenges

ISBN No.: 978-0-6928-2919-6

Edited by Lauren A. Ransome, Picture Perfect Page, 2016.

Printed in the United States of America

PREFACE

With unstinting honesty and eloquence, Samira L. Jones lifts the veil on two tragic events that women often experience with no voice and in silence: sexual abuse and divorce. She tells the story of her turbulent childhood, the joys and sorrows of her marriage, which ended in divorce, and how she emerged from the storm with a desire to show women that they too can create "sweet lemonade" from the tart rind.

In *Tough Skin: A Journey of Survival and Persevering Life's Challenges,* Samira L. Jones relates with her candor how at the age of 12 she experienced ongoing sexual abuse by her stepfather until he himself revealed to her mother the atrocities that were taking place. This tragedy was further exasperated by the revelation that once her mother found out, she did absolutely nothing. A confused and betrayed Samira was then abandoned by her mother, the one who should have been by her side, showing her the much-needed love and attention she had so desired her entire life, and left at the doorstep of her aunt where she continued to live until she became an adult.

She then describes in detail the courtship with her soon-to-be husband who impressed one of the most important people in Samira's life, her Uncle Johnny, whose great influence both on and in her life is paid homage. The courtship with her husband was exceptional in that he asked her out on their first date while she was obviously pregnant and the romance flourished, resulting in a 10-year marriage. She depicts her role as the wife and mother of a beautiful family who loved and greatly enjoyed being together—then, the walls started crashing down and no one but Samira could rebuild the foundation for her and her children. She speaks unflinchingly of the various stresses that she had to endure alone—her husband's affair, his ultimate estrangement from her, and the aftermath on her and the children.

As harrowing as Samira L. Jones's story is, her account is also uplifting. The inspirational author describes how she shook off the yoke of self-doubt, betrayal, and unhappiness, and provides women with a variety of tools for reclaiming their lives, including relationship survival tips, how to survive single parenting, rediscovering inner strength, and thoughtful, provocative questions that focus on identifying and facing fears and challenges and numerous strategies on how to move forward.

DEDICATION

I dedicate "Tough Skin" to all of those who saw something in me and reached out to support that young girl who was left behind to figure things out for herself; my Aunt Elaine, Aunt Bert, Uncle Johnny, and Unc's childhood friend, Ms. Olivia B. Washington, who today is one of my biggest cheerleaders; also to my children who will one day know their mother's story. I even owe this to my husband who even going through our divorce has made me realize that I am powerful. Those are five words that he spoke into my life in a prophetic way on several occasions saying, "You are a powerful woman." At the time, I did not know exactly what that meant and I never really sought to figure it out. It wasn't until recently during the last few years of being my Uncle's caretaker, going through the divorce process, and still continuing to be there for others in the midst of my own storm did I realize God knew what He was doing when He began this journey for me. He saw in me what I did not see in myself. Today, I stand stronger and bolder than ever, and now fully embrace that I am a powerful woman. Being powerful though, I cannot give myself all of the credit. A big part goes to those people who believed in me and took me under their wings and to all of you for that I am forever grateful and love you.

♡Samira

CONTENTS

INTRODUCTION

I wrote this book because *you* need it. What I have learned in this life is that everything that happens to us is for a reason, a season, and that my story did not happen to me for me; it happened for me to share. It happened for me to reach out and be a resource for people like yourself who are going through your own storm and are seeking hope, positive affirmations, and the confidence to move on after a disruption in your life.

Have you ever really wondered why is this life happening to me? Why can't I just get it right? When will the storm end? It just seems like one thing happens after the other, sometimes with a break in between, and for others it's a never-ending story. Well breathe, because this book will serve you well.

You will learn through real-life situations and short stories how to persevere the challenges of life. You will learn how to be okay with life happening to you, as you realize that it is really happening *for you*. Sounds insane right? Well guess what? Had I not taken took that journey of being okay with life happening to me, I *would* be insane!

What I do know today is that pains happen. You will experience more than your share of betrayals and painful situations if you are human. How we master the game of dealing with these issues is where many find the real problem. This book will force you to take a look from within and how you deal with situations. You will also read key tips to help you from going crazy in the midst of these challenges.

I am enough for whatever it is that life leads my heart to be and/or do. Being perfectly imperfect could be just what someone else needs from me.

CONFESSIONS FROM THE HEART

How I Got in My Own Way: My One Mistake

For several years, I would go back and forth with myself as to what to do about my situation in life, how to handle it, and how to address it. I questioned whether I should even share it, thinking that there was nothing unique about what I experienced. After all, who would care? I would also ask how anyone could benefit from it. This was my one mistake, not thinking that my story was enough to make an impact. Having this negative chatter allowed me to get in my own way.

You may often find yourself thinking the same thing or just not knowing how to use your stories and triumphs to help others. Make it your obligation to find out how. Someone out there needs to know how you made it through *your* storm. They need all of it, the good, the bad, and the downright ugly! Stop looking at what everyone else is doing, be a "doer," and get your own story out there.

Even if you are currently in a situation, share your experience while you are going through it. When you are able to do this, watch the magic happen! This is where things turned around for me. As you may already know, most successes come on the heels of a crisis in one's life. This is my story.

In 2014, my world fell apart when my family was unexpectedly shattered into pieces. My husband blindsided me with the ultimate deception. More on that later. For now, I just want to share how my road was laid out, as I was lost, confused, and did not know how I was going to bounce back from what I thought was a beautiful 10 years with the man I loved and family I adored, to now being abandoned by infidelities, lies, and betrayal. Who was I now? This is what had to be determined.

In March 2015, I attended the Steve Harvey conference, "Act Like a Success," which was held in Virginia and where my life would be forever changed. I literally had absolutely no idea why I was attending this conference. The only thing I knew at that time is that I needed some mommy time, as I had been enduring numerous challenges and changes during the continued transitioning of the separation. Of course, there were several guests and keynote speakers, none of which I had heard of before. The only person I was excited to get a glimpse of going in was Steve.

Let me tell you, what I walked away with from that conference was more than a glimpse of Steve. In fact, Steve was not who I was most impressed with. His keynote speech was great, but when I listened to Lisa Nichols and Doreen Rainey speak, life woke up in me again. I was *empowered!* I no longer looked at my situation as a misfortune, as it had now become an opportunity.

Doreen stood on that stage and stated how when we go through things in life, we hide from the world in shame and embarrassment. This was true. For several years, I had what I thought to be the damn-near perfect marriage. When it was realized that it wasn't, I experienced a feeling of hurt and wondered what *everyone else* would think. I removed myself from social media because I had a huge presence there. Everyone admired how so well put together my family was with the great husband and beautiful, intelligent children. We worshiped together, took trips together, and participated in the simple things like a lazy Saturday in the backyard grilling and playing with the children, which was our norm. That is all people identified our family with, *living the American Dream.*

So as I am sitting there in the conference listening to Doreen telling "ME" that I need to stop hiding and that people out there need to hear my story, I sat quietly in tears as everyone else seated in the room cheered Doreen's speech. It moved me so much that with tears flowing from my eyes and after 8 months of not being on social media, I reopened my account in the middle of the conference with tears flowing, telling my followers that I was back, and back to stay. I explained my departure and that my husband and I were no longer together. The tremendous outpouring of support was overwhelming, and that is when it started. I knew then what my purpose was and began to live in it.

It was my obligation to show others how to master the power of rejection, how to overcome it, and how to achieve a big bounce back. Even though I was still in my messy situation, I continued to move. As long as I could take intentional steps, no matter how small, I felt that I was accomplishing my goals.

I say all of this to say that you do not have to be perfect to serve others. Start now if you feel that is your calling. As embarrassing as it is to share, I will do so because being authentic will better show you that I am not only talking the talk, I have also walked the walk that I am speaking of to you.

While serving others in my current state of dysfunction, I not only did it in fear, I did it broke! I was helping others when I needed help myself. Many days I was only able to feed my children and not myself and sometimes with borrowed money. Sometimes, I would have an 8 p.m. conference call with the various members from my private online accountability group I created, as if there was nothing but roses in my back yard. One time my electricity was shut off. What did I do? I just took the kids to the library where they completed their homework and I performed work for my group members at the same time. What you're reading here is a pattern of perseverance. On Sunday, even in the midst of the hurricane season, I'd cheerfully give my last, because I knew that even though I was not understanding why what was going on was going on, I knew that it could be much worse and that I was still grateful for what I still had.

Did you know that helping others even when you need help yourself can actually be a blessed feeling? This selfless act empowers you through emotional satisfaction, which, in turn, turns into motivation to want more of that same feeling. When you feed yourself with that type of energy, you are feeding your mindset, which is the key component to making any change in your life. Your mindset is the golden egg that holds all of your keys to success, and without the proper mindset, there is no ambition to do more. Notice I did not say, want more, but *to do* more. You can want for all you want, but the ambition to actually putting forth action is where the results come in. So, get out of your own way in thinking that you are unable to move forward until your life is wrapped tight with a pretty red bow. Take action now, even if it is ugly. I promise you that the story is only temporary. You are enough!

Fear

During any crisis, fear is to be expected. What should not be accepted is staying there. You will read in my stories on how I opted to do things, become creative, shift my mind from dwelling in my circumstances, and transitioned into creating opportunities from them. You, too, must do the same. It will take sheer understanding and active intention to evolve from whatever it is that you are going through. The road will be lonely at times because no one understands better what you are feeling than you. To be honest, you will have to figure out the majority of it yourself. However, the great thing about that process is that you will pull from the experience, knowing yourself better than you ever have before.

Embrace the opportunity in front of you. This is your chance to show not only others, but more important you, to show just who *you* are. In comparison, as the environmental seasons change, seasons change in our lives. We are put in uncomfortable situations where we are forced to make decisions that will impact us and our families.

Don't be afraid of fear. Be afraid of what's not learned from the experience. You are in a vulnerable place in order to learn something. In those moments of silence, don't be afraid to face the only person in the entire room, *you*. Who will you discover in you? It is in these moments where often times our riches are found. As contrary as it sounds, it really is. Riches are more likely than not found in times of darkness. The darkness is the "it happened *to* me" chapter, and the riches are the "it happened *for* me" chapter.

Let me explain. When something happens *to us,* we battle with feelings of hurt, conflict, shame, sadness, and fear. We fear the unknown of the outcome. We do not know where the results of this situation will ultimately land us, so we are scattered into many pieces trying to figure out how to put the puzzle pieces together to make life whole again.

Riches come when we allow ourselves to be in that moment of darkness with full vulnerability, with nothing to hide, and with nothing to run from. The only way to discover your way out is to reveal what needs to be discovered, and that is you.

When my husband and I separated, I had to figure things out for *me* in order to move forward for *us.* The "us" includes the children, my husband, and myself. Initially, I had hidden myself because I was embarrassed that my marriage had failed. I was conflicted with the betrayal, and also at the same time, trying to figure out what life would be like without the man I had loved for all of these years. How was I going to move forward in a single-parent household, which I never had to do before? This was all new to me. I had to sit in silence, face my darkness, and fears. Expose the brick wall and piece by piece dissect the anatomy of your situation. What you will find is that most fear is not even about us. It is about the perception that we want others to believe. Some of these perceptions at one time may have been authentic, but at the end of the day, our lives should never be based or rely on the perceptions that other people have of us. Yet, the truthfulness of the life we live and the desire for ourselves is the only way to be authentic to who you are. Everyone else's perception is a non-factor.

Question: Name your top three fears that are holding you back. These are likely things that you really do not want others to know (the truth). What are you ashamed of? What are you not being fully honest with yourself about? Next, ask yourself what is the gain for me in leading these perceptions if any at all?

Last, ask yourself is it worth this much energy to protect?

_____

_____

_____

_____

_____

I affirm that from this day forward I will have a new lease on life! I will look at life from a different perspective of, instead of happening to me, it is happening for me.

DISRUPTION

When Life Pushes You Back

One thing is for certain, not a soul on this earth knows what lies ahead in their blueprint of life. "Life" happens to all of us. We make plans for ourselves that do not necessarily pan out the way that we expect. Such is Life.

Life attempted to push me back a few times. However, with a sincere commitment of being more relevant to myself than the circumstances I faced, I surprised life and a few of its minions along the way. I pushed back, and I achieved the big bounce back!

Life. This entity is defined in The Merriam-Webster Dictionary as, "the ability to grow, change, etc., and the experience of being alive." How do *you* define life? One may define life as the beginning (birth), until the passing of their earthly bodies (death). It is in this context we are going to use the term life as in the experiences that we have during the course of our living. Life happens to all of us.

We have tremendous memorable experiences, and we have experiences that negatively impact us for an indefinite period. Indeed, life can certainly bring on challenges.

Question: What three (3) major challenges are you facing right now? I want you to think about this for a moment before you start writing. What do you feel is weighing you down? What do you feel is keeping you up at night? What do you feel is not allowing you to propel forward? Be honest with yourself. This can only serve you if you are completely vulnerable and open with the one person who matters right now, which is *you*. Don't be a secret to yourself.

_____

_____

_____

_____

_____

Great, now here is my story (the first one anyway). I was destined for failure. Yep, life failed me from an early age. How? Well because I was faced with a challenge at a time when I was too young to be wise. I was not able to think clearly of a plan by stepping back, looking at the big picture, and figuring things out. My resolution at the time was to run away. Sound familiar? I'm sure that it does. As an adult, you run away from what is in front of you instead of dealing with it. As a child, I excused myself. As an adult, this way of remedying your issues is not at all acceptable. Nothing gets resolved when we sweep our problems underneath the rug, push them off, or act as if they do not exist. What does happen is that they mount into even bigger issues that eventually we will have to face down the road. Your various problems do not vanish when they go unaddressed. They become a silent pressure cooker. You *will* be forced to face the fire whether voluntarily or involuntarily.

So what was I faced with at such a young, vulnerable age when the only thing I should have had to worry about was school homework, tests, and friendships?

I was a 12-year-old child to be exact when I lost my innocence, my understanding of a mother, and my understanding of her purpose. I lost myself. During this period of my life, the man who had been my father at the time for 10 years was sexually molesting me. How did this change my life? I became an adult in what seems like overnight. It was almost like the story of the Baltimore Colts when the football team left Baltimore on the Mayflower overnight and absolutely no one knew. Something similar happened to me.

It was a warm spring day, as my mother was driving me to middle school when she asked me, "Samira, did David ejaculate in you?" she said. Understandably, being a 12-year-old, I had no idea what the word meant and had never heard of it until this day. "What does that mean?" I replied. "Did sperm come out of his penis inside of you?" You had to be a fly on the window to understand the confusion in my face. I had no idea why or how this conversation came about. She came at me straight out with it just like that. My mother had never been the loving mother type. She always had this wall up with her emotions and a coldness about her. This is just who she was. She confessed to me that my stepfather had informed her of what he had been doing to me and what took place most recently. The memory is as if it just happened yesterday, the night my mother left the house in tears on that rainy night. I never knew why she did and was told that she was going out for a while. As she drove away, I stood in the foyer and with my finger wrote on the fogged foyer window, "Mommy I love you."

At the time I had three younger siblings, one brother and two sisters. David's disposition was not of any concern as he initiated being in a playful mood and began to horse around with me and my siblings. Then it happened. I watched as David sent my siblings to bed and not me. He continued to play with me in his downstairs office, which also had a queen-sized bed in it. It was on the bed where he continued to toss me around. Of course, I thought nothing of it and just viewed the time as a daughter playing with her Dad.

Then, the door closed. The look in David's eyes was piercing as he approached me and became more gentle in his touch, which was far from the rough housing that had just took place. This was very awkward because I still was not processing what was about to happen to me.

This was the first time that I had experience in having oral sex. My stepfather placed his penis in my mouth and acted as if it was the greatest enjoyment of his life. I was sick as he held my head down and guided me in what to do for his satisfaction. As tears flowed down my face, it meant nothing to this monster. "Lay down" he said as he used his hands to offer assistance in laying me back on the bed. As I continued to weep, David pulled my pants down, placed a pillow over my face and demonstrated oral sex on me. All the while, my siblings were upstairs in their rooms in bed, my mother was gone, where to I had no idea. No one knew that I was being abused. No one knew that I was crying, torn, and being manipulated.

Then, I hear these words, "Let me show you what sex is like." No longer being able to take the torment, I jumped up, ran upstairs to my bathroom, quickly closed the door, and washed my mouth out, weeping, screaming, and crying for my mother.

There were many other times since that day that David approached me in the hallway when I would get up in the morning to get ready for school, sticking his tongue down my throat, or if I was eating in the kitchen, walk behind me and fondle my barely-there 6th grader breast. To my knowledge my mother had no idea at all that I was being taken advantage of in this way by her husband and that I was threatened not to tell her for if I did, I would lose my life.

When this was brought up to me that warm spring morning, I was confused about why he had mentioned it to her, yet relieved. I answered her question, "No," and was eager to think that she was going to take legal action and that this nightmare would finally be over. It was difficult going to school, as I was dreading when the school bell rang for me to go home. As my peers went home to loving families where they could actually be children, I faced a different story. I had to go home and be abused both mentally and physically.

Knowing that my mother now knew of this, I was not only relieved, I felt like I had the number one person on my side to whom I should have meant the world. We were going to nail this bastard! When she dropped me off that morning, she handed me $20, which I used to go to the mall with friends after school. My instructions were to be outside the front of the mall at a certain time, which I was. When she drove up, she was not alone nor was she driving, he was!

This was odd, given the situation and the conversation that had taken place earlier that morning. As I proceeded to get into the tan Astro van, I noticed my siblings laying in the back of it. There were no seats, but there were several black trash bags. I hopped in and everyone was quiet as we drove away. This ride was much longer than I expected. One hour turned into 2, then 3, then 4 before we ended up in East Orange, New Jersey, some place I never recognized visiting before.

It was late in the evening and we pulled up to this horror of an apartment building, which actually looked like a scene from Gotham City. My mother opened the side door to the van, told me to grab the trash bags, and to follow her. I still had no idea what was going on and that what was about to happen was going to take place. We rang a door bell to gain entry into the apartment building, and a woman's voice over the intercom who spoke to us let us in. As we were walking up the stairwell, I noticed a horrific smell and graffiti on the walls. After traveling up three flights, we arrived at the apartment. A woman who I had never seen before opened the door, and my mother and I proceeded to go inside. In all of 5 minutes, my mother introduced me to the woman who was identified as my Aunt G, who was the sister to my late Father, Jalail. I was told that this was my new home and then my mom left. Sounds unreal, right? Exactly.

So I was now a young 12-year-old whose parents just abandoned her. How do you deal with that? How do you process it all? What do you do?

I first had to understand that this was my situation, it was real, and I had to do the best that I could to accept it, not necessarily understand it, but accept it and deal with the cards I had been dealt. It was lonely, scary at times, and a time of survival for me.

Question: When life throws you a curveball, name one thing that you do to get a grip of your reality and to press on. What is your go-to (a bible verse, a friend or a family member, counseling)? What is the one thing that most serves you during a crisis and why?

_____

_____

_____

_____

_____

The one thing that serves me is finding a quiet place and going to a mental place of solitude. This is not to be excluded from others. The purpose of this is to meditate and be present with what I am facing so that I can then process, accept, and plan actions to take to move forward, in that order. We will discuss more on being present in section three. It is an essential component to truly being in a place of full awareness. When you are in full awareness, you are giving yourself a fair chance at maximizing your options to resolve the issue or situation that is facing you. Without full awareness, you are playing with a partial deck of cards and may not make the best choice possible to remedy the situation.

It's Not Your Fault

If you are reading this book as a survivor of domestic violence or sexual abuse, do know that what happened to you is not your fault. Give yourself permission right now to be free. Free yourself of the guilt, shame, embarrassment, and lack of confidence that you are holding within. Do not continue to be the victim by incarcerating yourself mentally because of someone else's illness. Yes, this happened to you, but guess what? Their issues are none of your business. Your business is to recover, to be well, to become whole again. Let me tell you, for years I tried to do everything I could to exploit this man and his wrongdoing. I felt that I had an obligation to the community, as he operated (and still operates) a community convenience store. I felt obligated to inform the neighborhood in which he worked and served several other young children who were the age I was when this all happened to me.

Being Abandoned by My Mother

It's difficult to receive a phone call from your mother, especially when calls were made so seldom, perhaps once a year or once every couple of years. To receive a call and be told, "Why don't you just go your way and I'll go mine?" as if she could just throw me away like I'm nothing—that hurts. I grew up so bitter and angry that I made poor choices. I recall times when I would just act out of anger that this woman allowed this to happen to me and that she was still with the man who did those horrific things to me. I would actually vandalize the store at times because I was angry and then the thing that would make me even more resentful and upset is when they would use that against me to tell my brothers and sisters that I was crazy, not telling them the truth about the real reason why I was doing what I was doing.

So, not only did I get betrayed by my mother who didn't protect me, they were turning my siblings against me, telling them that I was this bad person, that I was crazy, but that simply wasn't the case. The day that I walked into the store, I asked my mother's husband in front of my mother "Why did you do what you did to me"? When he responded, "Because you're not my daughter," my mother did absolutely nothing. I started thinking differently about her. I started to wonder, does she really know about that unforgettable night when I was sexually assaulted? Did he tell her that he was going to do that? To this day, this doesn't sit well with me. She did absolutely nothing when he said that. You would think as a mom that she would have slapped the hell out of him because he admitted to her what he had done to me. Then, to top it all off, she looked at me as if to say, "Okay, you got your answer now, so what are you still standing here for?" I went off! I walked outside, grabbed a trashcan, and threw it and some bottles into the store.

Unfortunately, to my siblings I looked crazy. There was a time where I was dating my college sweetheart. We stayed up one night talking because this really bothered me through the years. The fact that this man was a child molester not by accusation, but by experience, is out here in the street roaming freely and operating a business in a neighborhood that was full of children. A free man when he should be buried under the jail along with my mother. It wasn't until later that I realized that she's just as guilty. She was also a criminal because she was hiding this atrocity. One night we were sitting up and making flyers to take to the neighborhood to put on the doors. It was 1 a.m. in the morning when we posted these flyers in the neighborhood residences, on front doors, and in mailboxes when my mother's husband found out about it. He was furious. His late brother told me that he told him about it and that he said that when he sees me he was going to shoot my head off with a shotgun. His brother told him, "No, you won't." His brother is now deceased from a non-related, health problem.

It was difficult through the years. Not only did my mother fail me, the judicial system failed me as well. It's unfortunate that there is a statute of limitation for such a violation, which allows criminals to be free just because an allotted time period has lapsed. It's like, forget the crime...you didn't report it in a timely manner. Let me make this clear. As someone who has experienced sexual molestation, it is very difficult to come out about it when you're in it, especially at such a young, tender age of 12. I had an aunt who my mother actually confided in when she gave me away again, and she told her what her husband had done to me. When my aunt begged me to go to the police about it, I would get angry with her because I didn't even want to talk about it. This caused friction between my aunt and me even though she was just trying to help. It wasn't until later when I reached my mid-20's that I felt more confident to bring it to the board. Even then, I couldn't say certain words. I couldn't say that he made me have oral sex with him. That was very difficult for me to say. The system failed me. When my mother and her husband found out about it, they hired an attorney and made it difficult for the detective to come and speak to them about the incident. A detective visited my mother's school where she worked and asked to speak with her. She turned him away and never did return his call when he left a number. For several years, my mother has protected this man. I just don't understand the thought process behind a mother protecting a man who violated her child. Even so, through the years I still wanted her love, I still wanted her affection, and I still wanted somebody to call "mom."

The law failed me, my mother failed me, and my family failed me in my efforts. It was not until I was my 30's that I let go and I let GOD. So today, I come to you from a place of peace, a place of forgiveness, and a place where Samira needs to be in order to truly live for herself and her children.

Have faith that your higher power will carry you through the storm and that a new life awaits you when you decide to free yourself from that inner prison. The one thing I learned was that while I was sitting alone in disgust and holding onto all of the animosity, I wasn't holding anyone else back but myself. When I was spending time sulking in pain, it affected no one but me. As I was grieving about all of what I thought I had lost as a child, the very people who hurt me were moving on with their lives. They continued to be a part of society as if I had never existed, and they continued to raise my siblings, go on family trips, and live. So why should you suffer? You, too, must live. Give yourself permission to go through, get through, and live through! Be ALIVE!

You get one shot at this life. I'd be damned if you give it to someone else who does not deserve 1 second of your attention. Learn who are factors and non-factors in your life. When you understand the non-factors, you will see both your atmosphere and energy will change.

Being Present

Being present requires you to be in the moment, accepting and embracing *what is*. One way that just about everyone in the 21st century can identify with not being present is how we engage with our electronic devices, namely, our cell phones. Cell phones have taken over our lives for the last decade. With smart phones emerging, allowing us to do things quicker, faster, and better, we have become acclimated to an environment that wants everything yesterday and that is hyper sensitive to patience and to a society who has become unavailable to being present, being in the moment.

The various effects of this learned behavior transcend to other areas of our lives without our realizing it. When we go through a crisis, we should fully engulf ourselves to being present so that we can take full advantage of the resolution process. The following four steps are keys to helping us be present and to transition.

1. **Acceptance.** Immediately completely accept your reality so that you can address it. Frequently, we go into denial and do not want to accept what is really happening. More information on this will be covered in

"Relationships." Acceptance will allow you to be open to receiving.

2. **Figuring It Out.** After acceptance, you can be fully open to figuring it out, with "it" being your plan of action. This may require finding that place of solitude to think, reading some self-help books, or talking to close friends and family. You are never alone. I actually have found immeasurable and invaluable information in the self-help section of bookstores. You do not have to count your help out if you do not have people in your immediate circle to reach out to. That is why people like myself write books such as this. Help is out there to help you figure it out.

3. **Process a Plan.** Put a plan in place that will get you out of the funk. Put a plan in place that will give you your breakthrough to

move into a new light, a new season, and stick to it!

4. **Avoid Negative Chatter.** You are at a critical, yet sensitive time in your life where you want support. I myself learned this the hard way. Do not share everything with everyone. People will listen, but people will also spread negative chatter. Your words will become twisted and turn completely unrecognizable. Try to have discernment when choosing with whom to confide.

The Healing Process

Crises can be crippling, as they are a time of devastation, uncertainty, and weakness. Although the healing process can at times seem unbearable, it is a necessary undertaking in order to reclaim your life. Through my time of crisis, which occurred later in life and will be discussed in subsequent sections, I found comfort with implementing strategies that uplifted my spirit, including going to church; dining alone; being outside and embracing nature at the neighborhood park; and listening, watching, and feeding the birds to name a few. Find what makes you happy. Is this a real solution to long-term happiness? No, not at all. This is a great start to implementing "Happy Habits," which lead to other opportunities and ultimately long-term patterns of happiness. You have to start somewhere, so begin with what you know about yourself. Do those small yet large things in the big scheme of the picture, as this action will allow you to be open to more possibilities.

The healing process does not have to be a lonely one. Loneliness is a mental mindset position. You can, however, be by yourself and perfectly fine being by yourself and not feel alone. It is a great time to focus on you and not have to worry about the duty of focusing on others. Join some meet-up groups or a local volunteer organization in your community where you will be able to contribute and "give back." Community service is not only good for those individuals who receive, it is also extremely rewarding for those who serve. When my children and I had to start our lives over, we signed up for local charities and volunteered our service to help feed the hungry at the local food bank. Healing can be a time of exploration. Take advantage of its benefits!

Question: What activities bring you joy and how?

_____

_____

_____

_____

_____

Moving Forward

This time in your life can be bittersweet depending on the circumstances and nonetheless a part of the process that must take place, whether it is a separation from a relationship, a loss, or another traumatic event. Therefore, take advantage of this time to rebuild and to start fresh. In essence, take ownership of it.

Another reality of moving forward is that frequently you have to develop a *new norm.* In this story, I lost my mom, I lost my childhood, and I was forced to grow up prematurely at a rate most young girls typically do not experience. I still had to *accept* my reality, *figure out* how I was going to survive in my new surroundings without the family I once had, *process* a way to function, and *avoid* meaningless relationships and the wrong crowds.

Question: What are three ways you will move forward?

_____

_____

_____

_____

_____

Question: In what way will these strategies serve and support you?

_____

_____

_____

_____

_____

These questions are critical because you are building a systematic process to work through. It is my hope and intention to serve you through my words and for you to evolve through your own process.

Living in peace is a choice that I will make in order to live the best life possible for me. When I am at peace everything aligns with my spirit and purpose. Peace is the air I breathe.

LIVING IN PEACE

Having Peace of Mind

Living in peace first involves an understanding of what peace is, and how one practices peace is different for everyone. What we do have in common with peace is the feeling that one feels emotionally when they are connecting with peace. Being at peace is when you are able to find beauty in your life no matter what may be going on. For me, that peace comes from an intentional mindset that I want and *will have* peace in my life. It is that simple. When you make your mind up that that is where you firmly stand, then everything else that needs to align with that conviction will take place.

Peace for me is creating the atmosphere that I want to be in. For example, I love to light candles and sit in silence while I work or sometimes I may opt for a little soft meditation music depending on what I am working on and the mindset I need to be in for that particular task.

A change in atmosphere is another way to reboot and to be at peace. Creating a new space for peace is healthy and can help generate new, positive vibes. If you enjoy the outdoors, instead of sitting in the backyard all the time, go for a walk at the park and take in the beauty and life of a new environment. Peace can be reading a book. I have some great suggestions for reading located on my website at www.samirajones.com. Books, especially self-help books, are a great way to redirect your mind away from a negative state of being. When you are able to read success tips, advice on life strategies, etc., you are shifting your brain from being unfulfilled, to being empowered. There are many ways to discover what peace is for you. What is important is that the peace is meaningful in moving you forward in some way.

It is also very important to note that peace is what you *do not* allow in your atmosphere. Many people take this for granted but trust me, I don't. I am obsessed with being aware of what I do and do not allow to take shape in my life, which reflects on what we do and do not do from day to day. This either has a positive or negative impact on our mission in life, which all ties together.

This includes who you associate with, the type of music that you listen to, what gossip that you allow to be shared with you, what you watch on television, and so on. All of these contribute to your peace or lack thereof.

Ask yourself these questions:

What type of shows do I enjoy watching? Why? What do they do for me? What mood do they put me in when I watch them?

_____

_____

_____

_____

_____

What type of music do I enjoy listening to? Why?
What does it do for me? What mood does it put me
in when I listen to it?

_____

_____

_____

_____

_____

Who are my friends? What do they do for a living?
What do they enjoy doing in their spare time? Does
it align with what I enjoy doing? What in our
friendship serves me at this point in my life?

_____

_____

_____

_____

_____

What value do any of the above add to the peace I desire in my life?

_____

_____

_____

_____

_____

Who adds that value and who doesn't? How?

_____

_____

_____

_____

_____

What adds that value and what doesn't? How?

_____

_____

_____

_____

_____

Now, look at your answers. Do you see where there could be some additions and/or subtractions to your current situation? Be very aware of what is going in your life. It could be the small things that are the big changes that need to be made for you to make room for the availability to live in peace. Peace cannot co-exist with negative impacts.

Find Your Center

When you have disruption, the earthquake takes you off balance. How do you handle that? How do you find your center and again become grounded? It can be a very confusing and sensitive process where there is a thin line between having the spirit and energy to persevere or taking the less-challenging road, letting the chips fall where they may with no plan or ambition to conquer the storm.

"Within you, there is a stillness and a sanctuary to which you can retreat at any time and be yourself." -Hermann Hesse

You are your center. When faced with a time of hardship, you may have to do some work and take a visit on the inside and do what you may think is the unimaginable. Pull from your inner spirit.

When life is chaotic and throws us off course, we allow our external circumstances to define how we manage, often with the failing success of moving forward in anything we really need to be focused on and accomplishing to improve our mental caliber. When you are in this space, it is imperative to identify the object of distraction and start working on the solution to eliminate it from your atmosphere.

In one case, my husband had become very bitter during the course of our divorce. His bitterness had nothing to do with any actions of myself per say. It was all an internal struggle that he was having with himself. During our separation, he would intentionally go out of his way to create unnecessary discomfort to get a reaction from me. This ranged from removing my belongings from our home, taking them to the local police station, and stating that he did not want to have them in our home, to intentionally dropping off our daughter from the visitation late or not at all.

When people act in a manner to arouse you in a negative way, it is your job to not feed into that space. Find your center. Your center is a place that you can go for peace and comfort while the storm is in action. This could be scripture, a place of serene surroundings, reading a great book, treating yourself out to dinner, calling a good friend up, or even planning something fun to do with the kids. Breathing exercises are also great, as studies show that deep breathing can reduce blood pressure and send signals to the brain to subside stress and anxiety. Deep breathing is a form of meditation that can have a great impact on your ability to cope. So gravitate to those things that encourage you to make healthy choices, the things that destress you when in a situation that can otherwise be highly stressful.

Your center is a special place that should be held in high regard. For many their center is all they have. Their center is what keeps them going. If you are unsure of what your center is, look at the patterns in your life when you are in situations that take you away from yourself. What do you typically do? Who do you typically tend to lean on for support? Where do you go?

Fill Up Your Cup

You deserve a life of abundance and for your cup to be full. How you fill your cup up depends wholly on how you view what is important to you. My cup is full when I have a dose of Jesus, when my children are happy and healthy, when I can fulfill my daily to-do-lists, have peace and harmony all around me, and when I can have a positive impact on others. Having a full cup is the equivalent to having a full balance of self. It is simply those important things in your life that make up who you are when you are most happy. Is your cup full? You must live each day with purpose to understand what this even means. That purpose is to discover what puts you in a place where you are living your best life.

How you view what is happening in your life determines how you react to it. There are so many opportunities that I can name where I could have reacted in a way that would not have served me. I will admit that there were times before when I did do that, and this is how I can speak from a place of experience. Therefore, once I learned that my reactions to those situations emptied my cup, I began to reconsider how I choose to respond. My hope is that you understand that filling your cup is a choice and a responsibility that is yours to discover. What fills up your cup?

What I Know for Sure

Today, what I know for sure is that life itself does not promise us anything. The promise comes from within who we are. The promise comes from how we view ourselves, our environment, how we process it all, and release it into the atmosphere. We are our promise. Situations will take place during the course of our lives as long as we have breath and air to breathe. Although we cannot control what others place into the atmosphere for us to deal with, we are the keeper of our own promises.

There will be disappointment for sure, but the learning curve is how you grow from your pains instead of placing blame on them. Look at your setbacks, heartbreaks, betrayals, and all of your other circumstances as opportunities. In everything we experience there lies an opportunity to adapt, to be the change, or to make a difference in your life as well as others. This is what my mission was when deciding to write this book. I wanted to share my story not to place blame on the actions of others, but to share how I took situations that could have turned out very differently if I had not responded differently and honored the promise to myself.

From an early age, even when I did not understand why I was going through what I was going through, being treated the way that I had been treated, I did know that there had to be something greater out there for me. I knew that I did not want to follow the wrong crowd, and certainly prove right to the nay-sayers. Failure was never an option for me. That was the promise I stood on and the promise that brought me here at the age of 36 years old to write this book and help you.

Let go of the hurt. Let go of the blame. What I know for sure, is that it will never serve you and your promise. When you look at life differently, you view life differently and do things differently. I take no moment for granted. Just recently while driving, I was showing my children the beautiful autumn trees. We often look up and admire the skies. Then I show them the people who are driving and focusing on getting to their destinations. So many people miss life even though they are living right in it. Take life in slowly, touch it, smell it, embrace its gift to you. What I know for sure is that you will begin to view the world through a different lens. The obvious won't necessarily seem so obvious anymore. A tree no longer will be just a tree. The rain won't be just rain. You will begin to find an appreciation in all of those things that we tend to see every day or not see because we take them for granted. Breathe, inhale deeply and exhale slowly, the goodness of all that surrounds you. What do *you* know for sure?

_____

_____

_____

_____

_____

I have decided to embrace any challenges and changes and release all feelings of inadequacy. I will retain my good mood through all things and retain a healthy attitude through all adversity!

BOUNCING BACK FROM DECEPTION

One of the most dreadful situations that one can imagine within a marriage is divorce. This is especially true when you have built so much together between the two of you. Not just the external factors, but the bond—something bonded you together that made you want to get married. When divorce is even a thought, it hurts on *both* sides because of the confusion and the uncertainty of life itself and where it leads. For me, it felt like death; however, my personal scenario may be a little different. In most divorces, both people see it coming, but I didn't. My husband had emotionally abandoned our relationship way before he decided to physically abandon it. It wasn't until I was still and allowed God to open my eyes, which allowed me to rest and to be quiet. It was in those moments, when there was nothing but silence surrounding me and I could listen, that I became conscious of the fact that I had been living in deception. The one thing that I will emphasize is that when you have a

54

union, and a family and children are involved, it is your responsibility to your family to exhaust *all options* first before deciding to make such an impactful decision based solely on what you are feeling. They deserve that and just as important, you deserve that. Sometimes this may mean seeking professional help. Friends are great to talk with, but when you're making such a life-changing decision, I recommend speaking with someone who is neutral and not a part of that relationship. When you don't do that, it's a selfish act because then it becomes only about you and no one else involved is considered. This was something that I had to bounce back from. Yes, initially, when I heard those words I experienced a slow death. I just didn't understand what was happening and none of it made any sense to me. Again, when most people are at that point and hear those words, they can go back and say, "Well, I did see it coming to this, and I knew this would be the end result." I couldn't say any of that, so it just didn't make any sense to me.

What I had to do immediately, however, was accept that this was my reality and figure out a strategy of how I was going to move forward from this not only for myself but for my children as well. Our children were involved, we have a home together, they are schooled, and this was a lot. But, then that peace that I love to speak about—that peace that God puts over you in the midst of a storm—came to life and that peace is what let me know that I would be OK, the children would be OK, and the peace allowed me to look at my circumstances differently. Instead of me perceiving my circumstances as a failure, I started to think of all of the little things that had recently happened, which added up and gave me that "Ah ha" moment. It was from those various things I became comfortable with where we were because I realized at that point from adding all of those "insignificant" incidents that I ignored or didn't think much of contributed to where we ended up. I then turned both my fear and the feeling of the "death of my marriage" to gratitude. How do you do that? You accomplish this by being still, allowing life to happen, and letting it happen in a way where it doesn't affect you in a negative manner yet affects you in a way that makes you think, which is what it did for me. It made me think about the fact that this is not a person I feel would have my best interest at heart or who I could trust. Just those facts alone turned into gratitude because I no longer had that individual in my life.

So, you *can* shift where you are. It's all mental and begins with *you.* Once I was able to realize that, as stated previously, I viewed my circumstances differently and from a perspective of gratitude and then began to build. The gratitude is what moved me forward. This is also what opened up new relationships and allowed me to meet new people who were like-minded and to form a community of support, which ultimately led to writing this book, starting my mentoring program, and coaching other women who were experiencing adversities in their relationships. I was determined to turn what could have been something extremely negative to something positive in my life. It's all about perspective, mindset, and intention. It is important for you to note that when I say intention, I mean be *intentional* about how you want to live your life. I refused to be down in the dumps. When I say refused, I mean *refused*! It has just never been in my makeup and I've been through quite a bit up to now. Although it has never been in my make up to be a victim of my circumstances, my marriage was not an exception. Today because of my perseverance I am willing to move forward and not stay stuck. I am now known as the "Bounce-Back Strategist," helping women such as yourself or women you know bounce back in a way where they are developing healthy relationships with themselves in a fantabulous way. So if you take anything from this, please take this one very important message. God does not take you through any door that closes shut and does not open another one. Realize that you are a part of that process. However, you have to continue to have faith, put one step in front of the other in an *intentional* way that you want to live the best life for yourself, and continue to have gratitude. Even in the midst of the storm if you do that, I guarantee you that you'll be taken care of.

The Husband I Thought I Knew

Betrayal can be one of the most difficult things to understand, especially when you do not see the signs of it. For 10 years, I was with a man who I thought loved me unconditionally. I know that I'm not perfect, but who is? Ten years later I realized that what we had was not what I thought we had. I met my husband in 2004 when I was pregnant with my son and we worked together. One day I was walking to the vending machine because I was hungry and experiencing the munchies caused by the "pregnant syndrome." I was about 7 months pregnant and I was bending down to get some Cheez-It crackers, which was one of my pregnancy cravings. There was a gentleman behind me who said that that he would get that for me. I turned around and the person informing me that he would "get that for me" was who became my husband.

How we met was unconventional. Most men don't end up asking a woman out when they see that she is pregnant, as it is assumed that she is in a relationship. Regardless, I saw him and thought that he was a nice-looking guy, so I pursued him. He worked as a building mechanic at my job. One day, I got clever, called down to the office where he worked, and told his supervisor that he left his tools at my office. When he came to the office and asked about his tools, I turned around with my phone number in hand and said, "Here they are, make sure that you use them." He looked at me and just smiled.

After he left, that evening I received a call from him and we spoke all night until we both had to return to work on Thursday. I had invited him over for breakfast that Saturday when he showed up at the door dressed up, wearing dress shoes with a buckle, and in his hand were white roses. The romantic gesture is something that would have surprised me for a dinner invitation; but, for breakfast? I graciously accepted the beautiful roses and jokingly asked him where he thought he was going so dressed up. I told him that he didn't have to come over dressed up like that just for breakfast. We had a good time! We ate breakfast, sat on the couch, and talked. This afforded the both of us with an opportunity to get to know a little more about one another, and we both discovered that we love Häagen-Dazs ice cream. We ended up going to Georgetown in the heart of Washington, DC, to the Häagen-Dazs store, and what a fantastic experience that was! As we were walking down M Street, mind you, I'm pregnant. As you may know, Georgetown is very quaint and the streets are tight so the sidewalks are small. Therefore, he's guarding my stomach as people are walking by. When we were in the store folks started to congratulate us on the pregnancy. His "thank you" was uncomfortable because of course this was not his child and I did not know how to accept that. From here, we created an excellent friendship that eventually turned into a romantic relationship. Then, in 2005 we had our daughter. The relationship I had with my husband at that time definitely had successfully transitioned into something very special.

The following year we built a home, and my family was everything to me. I adored my husband so much that every morning when he would leave to go to work, I always looked out the door or window until I couldn't see his tail lights anymore. I would just say, "I love you," and pray to God to keep him safe, going to and from work. We were the type of parents that showed up at our kids' school. My husband would fly to where our oldest son lived with his mom in Louisiana to support him at his school events and did the same thing when they lived in Michigan. Likewise, locally we were always attending school functions and we were parents who showed that we cared deeply about our children's education. So, when did all of this go so wrong? That's an excellent question and an answer that I still haven't been told to this very day. It was July 18, 2014 and my husband woke up next to me. We chatted for a little bit and he said to me that he was going to take our children to the movies. Of course, I was okay with that, as I was working at home. Later that afternoon when he returned home, I received the text message, which read, "I love you, and I miss you. You owe me 222 hugs and kisses, T.J."

Now, I was never one to check after my husband. I had never checked his phone nor gone through any of his personal items while we were married and never felt the need to. I really felt that this man was of faith and integrity and... that he genuinely loved me. So, I didn't think anything of it. I just replied in a joking kind of way, "Oh, this must have been meant for T.J.," not even meaning anything by that. I really was kidding around. He replied right back to S.J. for my initials. After I received his reply, I continued to work until I left the house and drove to get some crabs, which I love! When I returned, I asked if he wanted some crabs, and I sent the kids upstairs and told them to tell their dad to come downstairs to get some. I was sitting and eating the crabs outside in the gazebo. Eventually, he came downstairs, the children were in the gazebo and they ended up going inside to play. I then asked my husband if he wanted to go with us for a ride to the beach the following day, which was Saturday. He shook his head no, and the look in his eyes was very different. I didn't understand why he answered the way he did, as his response was very different from the way in which we usually communicated. We always had a very loving relationship and respected one another, so I thought, and it was how we raised our children.

Finally, I ended up asking him if there was something wrong because I just wasn't used to him communicating in this way. We didn't have any immediate issues at that time, and therefore I couldn't think of any reason why he would respond to me in that manner. He stated that he didn't like what he saw when he looked in the mirror at himself and that he didn't like where he was in life. He told me that he thought I was a great mom, beautiful, powerful, and that I was going to do great things in life. This went on for about 15 minutes before I asked where he was going with this and he said to me, "I love you. I just don't love you the same." and of course I was still not getting it. He then said, "I think we should go our separate ways." My crab dropped. I was literally waiting for Ashton Kutcher to pop out from somewhere because I was not expecting that at all. Of course, I looked stunned and asked him why. He could not give me a reason. He just said that he felt we had grown apart. I sat in that gazebo with him for hours, 3 hours to be exact trying to get him to consider seeing a counselor to maximize all of our options before giving up just like that. After all, we had a beautiful family. We just sent our eldest son off to college and gave him a graduation party in May.

There just wasn't anything that I felt could not be discussed and if necessary if seeing a counselor would help, I was willing to do anything to try and keep our marriage together. As you can imagine, Friday was extremely difficult and we ended up hugging. He was crying and I was crying; it was surreal. It wasn't as if he had told me that he hated me. He just didn't want to be together anymore. I must have been the worst person ever and stormed out of the house. It really was the strangest separation conversation I had ever even heard of and we ended up going inside the house. It was late, we took a shower together, he washed me up, and I washed him up. Again, he hugged me. I still did not believe that I heard what I just heard. Then, we laid and I cried the entire night wondering why this was happening to me and to us and what was going on. I tried to talk to him but he appeared to be in a very dark space, just quiet. The next day was Saturday, and I was at a point where I was trying to do all that I could to figure this out. I gathered pictures out of my office of the children when they were younger. I got these boxes out and grabbed my laptop because I share so much of my life on Facebook—I wanted him to see that and to see the love that we've had through the years for us, our children, our family, all of the gatherings that we would have, just everything about our life that we loved.

I asked him if he would come with me to the park, which is right on the bay has stunning views. We loved going there to go fishing as well as taking the children. I wanted him to go somewhere away from the house where we could be in a completely different environment, the type of environment that we actually enjoyed as well outside of the home. I was just trying to figure out what was going on, so I showed him all of these pictures and he just kept saying that he had to leave, then he started crying. He was holding onto me and tears were streaming from his eyes. Again, he said that had to go. It was really difficult, and even after hearing this we stayed at the park for a couple of hours before leaving.

I spoke to him about me taking out a loan to help catch him up on the house payments that he hadn't paid in months, because I did not want him to further ruin his credit. I was really concerned for him. I even said that I would not take him for child support so that he could get himself together. My initial intention was to really be there and support him for what I felt was a midlife crisis. This of course was before God revealed the truth of the matter.

What was even more strange was what he said next. He told me, "Do not get too close to anyone because I'm coming back for you." I mean really! Are you serious? He then said, "If anyone asks what happened between us, I will tell them that we had a good ride." Me, (blank stare). So yes, I was completely convinced that something was not right with my husband. Something or someone had taken over his mental stability!

When we exited the park, we decided that we were going to get something to eat and as we walked away we were holding hands while walking to our car. It was such a somber day and such a somber moment. After we got something to eat, we noticed that my tire was receiving a low-air signal. We stopped at a tire store and he bought me a new tire for my car. While we were waiting for the tire to be replaced, he just pulled me closer and hugged me. This was just the strangest situation.

No-one would have ever thought that we had the conversation that we just had, yet he still was convinced that he wanted out of our marriage.

When we returned home, the children were playing and of course we had to act as if none of this had happened. They were not aware of what was about to happen with their mom and dad. They were not aware that the family that they've known and that life as they knew was about to be changed forever. As you can imagine that entire day I was in the fog, asking God what was going on. I didn't understand. Later that evening we actually made love. He looked into my eyes and I looked into his. Again, I was sad not understanding or having a clue about what was happening to us and why. One of the things that he did say was that he was unhappy, but there was no explanation. This is one of the hardest things to understand or at least to try to begin to accept; when someone is not forthcoming or they only give you a part of the story. I told my husband that it was very unfair of him to simply tell me that he wasn't happy without providing any type of explanation. I also told him that it was selfish, particularly when he had a family and because he was in a crisis he wasn't considering the other lives that were are going to be impacted by his decisions. It was also unfair when a vow is taken before God to honor one another until death do you part, all of which was dismissed when he was having feelings about something that he was not willing to try and professionally have addressed. When I asked him about us seeing a counselor, his response was, "If we have to go to a counselor, then we definitely should not be together." Of course, that simply was not true.

One thing I know for sure is that in any relationship people grow, which means that change is inevitable. Whenever you grow, that's change, and if you're not growing, and you're not changing, then something definitely is wrong. Now the caveat to that is that when you grow and change, sometimes that growth isn't exactly in sync with the other person the way that it was when you were at a different world stage in life. At the same time, as we evolve, and change as people do, it is our responsibility to recognize that change and to be accepting of the reason. Many men complain that in marriages the sex declines or that things don't happen the way that they used to. However, in my opinion that is not a valid reason to divorce because if that was the reason you married, then you married into deception. People change. People's chemistries change, and people's health change every day. Stresses changes people, but that doesn't mean that you just give up. One thing is for certain. No matter what relationship you're in, people are going to change. If you're in relationship just for the bliss of it all, then you're being unfair to the person who you told that you love, because that's not love. Love doesn't fade over the gradual ebbs and flows that are experienced in relationships. No matter what relationship you're in, things are going to get dull especially when you've been in a relationship for a long time. If anyone says that it doesn't, then they are lying. You're going to have differences, but when you love each other you work them out. That doesn't mean that the person doesn't love you anymore or that the person doesn't respect you or that there just isn't any hope. You simply can't run away from any problems that occur in a relationship. Every relationship will experience something at some point in time, and you can't continue to run and look for the next best thing because that next best thing is only going to be that for so long again.

Look for ways to be creative. Instead of feeding the emotion of what lost your feelings, feed the power of love with faith, with guidance from God and with the initiative to keep the fire burning. That's what makes relationships special, when you're able to realize that it's not going to be perfect, when you're able to realize that as the years go by we took this vow to be together until death do us part. I know things are going to change with you. You know things are going to change with me but at the end of the day and no matter what, I love you and you love me. That's what's missing in many relationships today. People really don't understand or value the secrecy of marriage. They get in because it feels good and they get out because that feeling has been buried somewhere. Life happens especially when you have kids, who change everything. We may love them dearly, but having children changes things. This is why you must carve out time for you and your spouse. I would always take us on trips. For example, I would book a family trip or book the trip out of the country for my husband and me. I would do things to show him that I love him by leaving little notes on his sink or in his lunch. If he had a long day at work, I would drive down the highway and call him up when I knew he was driving home, which was about a 90-minute drive home. Depending on the traffic, I would say, "Hey, stop off at the Outback. I'll be there waiting for you." I would then have a beer sitting on the table waiting for him when he walked in.

Doing little things like those described above display love. My husband never had to worry about cutting the grass, as I often did this so that when he drove home from work he could relax and not have to worry about that chore. If it was snowing outside, he would often want to do it. If I got up before him, I would do it. If he was shoveling the snow, I would make certain that when he walked back into the house that a nice hot bath was waiting for him to warm him up. In addition, while he was outside, I would bring him hot tea to drink. It's the simple things like that which show love. So again, I really just did not understand this weekend at all. That Saturday night after we made love, my husband told me that he had to leave and that he was going to stay at a hotel for a few days. He informed me that he would return the next week. This was one of the most confusing and hardest things that I've ever had to deal with because I had to remain emotionally together for the kids and at the same time dissect what my reality was. In fact, that's one of the things that my husband said to me, that this is my reality and that I needed a fresh start. What did that mean? I had no idea? I didn't ask for a fresh start. On Sunday, I knew that he would be at work and I went to his job because I wanted to see him. When I arrived, he had already left work for the day 2 hours early. The following day, which was a Monday, I tried again, and this time I ordered an Edible Arrangements and a bouquet of flowers to let him know that I was thinking about him.

I showed up and the security guard called him. He came out to meet me at my car. When he sat in the car, we talked. I expressed to him how much that I loved him, that I didn't know what was going on, and that I didn't understand why he was in this space. He never said that it was anything that I did to him personally. He just said that he felt that we had grown apart. When I asked him to reconsider attending counseling, his echoed his previous words that if we needed someone else to come into our relationship to resolve our problems, then we really didn't need to be together. I just didn't understand that. He did eat the Edible Arrangements and offered me some. We sat there, ate some fruit, and had a conversation. I repeatedly told him how much I loved him and asked when he was coming home. He told me tomorrow, which was Tuesday, and that he had another night at the hotel he was staying at so I said okay and I returned home. He did return on Tuesday and the children, who were extremely excited to see him, greeted him at the door. I was excited as well and just happy to have him home even though we were in the dark place that we were in.

When he returned home, things were certainly different. I really couldn't piece together any of this. It wasn't until I contacted the pastor of my church, who had just baptized us the week before, and told him what was going on that everything came to a halt and surfaced. When I contacted the pastor, gave him the details of what had just happened, and asked him to please speak to my husband, he said, "You know, I hate to plant this seed in your head. However, it sounds to me as though the problem could stem from infidelity from the experiences that I have had with other couples in my office over the years." Being naïve and still living in the past of the husband who I thought I knew, I immediately dismissed infidelity as an option. I thought about it after we got off of the phone and did something that I never felt the need to do, which was to check our phone records. When I contacted Verizon, they gave me access to the account and lo and behold, there was an out-of-state number that I had didn't recognize with several entries over the course of several months. Whomever this individual was, he or she had very long conversations with my husband, which spanned from 1 to 2 hours and many of the calls occurred at 4 a.m. in the morning when he would leave for work. They were doing much of their talking during lunchtime, which is also when he would come out to his car and make these calls because he worked at a secure facility and why he could not have his phone in the building. The most startling part is that he would have conversations with this person as soon as he would get off work and during his 1.5- to 2-hour drive home and then the calls would end when he would arrive home.

So who was this person? I had to find out, which was not a difficult thing to do given my background as a private investigator. What I found was that this was the phone number of another woman. When I discovered this information, I immediately became numb. At that moment that's when it all made sense. The text message that I received on July 18, 2014 was certainly not meant for me; it was meant for this other woman. Now everything added up. Everything finally began to come clear that I was in a whirlwind of pure deception and it did not end here. Once I found out about the other woman, I contacted a friend of mine and it was surprising to her as well because, again, everyone looked to us as "the model couple." This could not be happening to us, but it really was. I did not call the number and I did not call my husband. My girlfriend actually offered us her home that she had on the market to stay at to get my head cleared because she just couldn't imagine the pain that I was feeling—and she was right. I took her up on her offer, gathered the kids, and as we were leaving ran into my husband at the door. As we were walking out and he was walking in, I played off the situation because I did not want to bring the children in the matter. I just told him that we wanted to go out for a while to give them a break, letting him relax, and we left. That night knowing that I was not going to return back home, I felt obligated to at least let him know that we were okay and that we were just going to get a room for the night. I sent him a text letting him know that I was going to take the kids out so that he could have some alone time and enjoy his weekend. He never replied.

The following day I received an alert from the alarm company, which was tied to my e-mail whenever we arm or disarm the home. Our house was armed early in the morning, but it was never disarmed in the evening, which definitely told me something—he did not come home. So, when he didn't return home again things were becoming more clear. This wasn't about me, and that's why he couldn't say anything to me about me. This was about him not being able to face his own deceit and sin. It was about 3 a.m. when I woke up out of my sleep and something told me to drive to that address. I arrived about 1 hour later, and there it was, the TRUTH! I pulled up to this woman's house in the middle of a dark summer night, and my husband's car was parked in front of her home. It was confirmed. I drove off, but my spirit was different now. My spirit was peaceful and I actually did not have a tear to shed. I felt God's protection over me at that moment because God knew that I had tried to do everything that I could to save our marriage. I gave my husband every opportunity to help us fix this and because of that I believe that God had grace in my life and protected me from feeling shattered. He put me in mission mode.

On August 1st, I drove to the county circuit court and filed for divorce. After I filed for the divorce something told me to go back and obtain evidence. At this point, I had contacted another girlfriend and let her know that I needed pictures of this for court, and that it was my intention to do just that. Where I did go wrong was that I had the children with me because I was running off emotion and not clearly thinking, which obviously was not the best decision on my part. I was in a state of shock and not understanding why things were happening the way that they were. After I filed for the divorce and later met up with my girlfriend, we drove up to this woman's residence. As soon as we pulled up to take pictures, in less than 30 seconds later my husband pulled in behind us with her in the car. He did not recognize me because I was in a different vehicle. I was recording everything. A couple of minutes later, he got out the car with this woman and walked with her to her door. That's when all hell broke loose, and the situation got the best of me. As you're reading this book, I know you're probably wondering how in the world did I hold tight for so long up to this point and can probably understand why I broke. I got out of the car. As I approached him while he was walking to her house I said, "So, is this the reason why you want us to separate? Is this what's really going on?"

He pushed her into her home and closed the door in my face! Yes, you heard me right. My husband of almost 10 years turned his back on me, walked into another woman's house, and closed the door. That is when the pulse came out and I started knocking on that door, ringing the doorbell, and reminding him that he was my husband, not hers. I also said that whoever she was it didn't matter to me but that he needed to come outside and explain this.

Eventually, he opened up the front door, came outside, and went on a tangent that this woman was just a friend and that she's been friends with him for 30 years. Come again? Yes, as if this was okay, as if this was excusable, as if this was a valid reason for him to be at another woman's house. After he came outside another gentleman appeared behind him and asked if he could explain the situation to me. I told him sure. He introduced himself to me, told me who he was, and that my husband is a childhood friend of his. He stated that my husband went to pick up his cousin from the bus station and that her name is Yolanda. This is a true story and, yes, this really happened. I had to stop him at that point because he was obviously involved in all of the deception as well. "Apparently, my husband did not tell you that I spent years as a private investigator and that I already know who she is. I know her name, I know whose house this is, I know of everyone, I know the owners, and I knew what she looked like before I even arrived. Therefore, I know that that is not Yolanda. If you would please excuse yourself and let me finish handling this with *my* husband, I'd appreciate it." Of course, that shut him down and he went back inside. I continued talking with my husband and letting him have it because he lied to me, he lied to our family, he deceived me, he deceived our family, and *we did not deserve this.*

He tried to justify something that could not be justified. As he was leaving, the gentleman came out of the door and they drove off in his car. I was furious! I went into my husband's car, took some of his precious belongings, and then drove off with my girlfriend. All of a sudden, something hit me and I know that it was God who told me, "Samira, this is not even worth it. This is really not you. It's going to be okay. It's all going to be okay." I then told my girlfriend that this wasn't me and that I just wanted to give him his things and move on with my life. She agreed that that was the best thing to do. We turned around on the highway and went back to the neighborhood that we just left from, but my husband had not returned. This time, two women emerged from the home where my husband and this other woman were seen entering. They walked over to our vehicle I'm sure wondering why in the world we had returned. Immediately, I apologized letting them know that I was not in my right character and for bringing that situation into their neighborhood, but that there was something that they needed to understand. I did not know the woman who they called their mother. Even though she and my husband claimed to be friends for 30 years, she was not a friend in our marriage. I then explained that I had never heard of her and they understood. In addition, one of them specifically said that she knew how it felt to be cheated on and revealed that the other woman has PTSD. Therefore, if she saw me when she came back, it could be a problem. As she was explaining this, the other woman drove up and one of the young ladies approached me and informed me that I should get back into my car because if she sees me, she's going to think that I came to the neighborhood to cause a problem. Then she said, "Hold on. I will go tell her that everything is okay." Therefore, I did that and as the other woman approached me, we began to have a talk. This conversation actually developed into an almost 3-hour-long talk. The conversation first started with me apologizing for my actions, then explaining that I did not know who she was or why she was involved in my marriage. This is when it took everything for me not to explode.

She Was Just a Friend: The Other Woman

As Tcee (the other woman) was approaching, I let her know the reason why was there. I told her that I came back to bring my husband his belongings and to apologize for my behavior. I told her that I knew nothing about her, and that my husband a few days before had left our family without any explanation. Then, I find him at her home, spending the night. Tcee went on to say that she has been friends with my husband for 30 years, that she knows his entire family, and that she was just being there for him. Yes, she said that she was just being there for my husband even in the state of confusion, anger, and shock that I was in. I was able to suppress all of those feelings and allowed her to speak. She was certainly out of place telling me that she was being there for my husband, no matter what their relationship was. What I did have to tell her was that she may have known my husband for 30 years, but that she was certainly not a friend in our relationship. What I also went on to tell her is that a real friend would have told him to take his married behind home and work out his issues with his wife instead of laying up with him and giving him a roof over his head in her home. A real friend would not do that. She went on to say that he had disclosed our financial issues and then she proceeded to ask me why I was not paying half of our mortgage. At this point, I clearly had to suppress all of the feelings inside of me to avoid thunder slapping this chick.

First, she disrespected me by telling me that she had been there for my husband and second, questioning me about our marital business. I went on to tell her that since she was so aware of our marital arrangement that in the 9 years that we lived in our home I had never paid the mortgage as it was not my responsibility nor what my husband had arranged when we purchased our home. When my husband carried me across the threshold of our new home, he said that the home was a gift to me and to our family. He also said that he would pay the mortgage, and that I would take care of the other bills, such as the utilities, etc. I was really trying to avoid coming off as the bitter wife, even though I had every right to be, because I had been blindsided by my husband. What I did tell her was that if she knew that much, then she must know how he had stopped paying the mortgage that entire year and how our house was $20,000 dollars behind in the mortgage. There was no reason to be this far behind because my husband was a six-figure earner. Then she got quiet before she said, "Well, then you're stupid because wouldn't no man be living up in my house and not paying the bills." Again, suppression. It took everything in me again to not thunder slap this chick because it went from her being there for my husband to her questioning me about our finances, to her telling me how I should respond when our bills aren't being paid. I answered her in the best way that I could at that time and I said, "I'm not going to give up on my husband just because of his irresponsibility and again that's our marital business. But since you know everything, I just figured that we are having a conversation about the things you already know, since apparently with your being there for my husband, you know everything."

As stated previously, we continued talking for about 3 hours and by this time I really was not even concerned or upset at the fact that he had betrayed me for this woman. Why? Because I saw what a downgrade he had chosen. Once I realized how ratchet this chick was, I knew for sure that this was not going to be something that my husband would be involved in for long-term. Unfortunately, he made this decision, and I was ready to roll with it. Just like that God had protected my heart because He knew what was going on and that this was the time that He had to show me, even if it hurt. Father God had to show me that I was not being treated with respect in my marriage and that there was no integrity on the part of my husband.

It had only been 1 week earlier that I was negotiating with him because I was trying to be supportive, even when he wanted to leave our family, and told him that I would take out a loan so that the house could get caught up. So even though he was leaving us, I did not want that to be on his credit. Now mind you, I did not have to do that because it would not have affected my credit since his name was on the loan. I did this out of the kindness and the love in my heart for the man that I vowed to love til death do us part. I even told him that I would not take him to court for child support that I wanted him to get on his feet. I really felt at that time, not knowing that it was another woman, that my husband still needed my support even though he did not want to be married to me any longer. It was just so real then to find out that it really was another woman. So before I did that and I really did make a big mistake, God had to stop me in my footsteps and show me what was really going on.

Back to the evening of August 1st, where I'm speaking with Tcee outside of her home. We eventually began to speak cordially and the conversation became less formal. She did ask me one thing. If he didn't want me anymore, why wouldn't I just let him go? Again, my reasoning was none of her business and for her to ask me that was inappropriate. By the end of the laborious 3-hour conversation, I had spoken with my husband on the phone, on her phone by the way. She called my husband on her phone because he had already changed his number and she had it, and I did not. Therefore, she gave me her phone because I would not give her his security badge and his belongings without his authority and approval. Once I received this, I gave her his things and before we left, she and the young women gave me a hug. They also let my children use their restroom before we got back on the road and that was the end of the night. As we drove away, I felt a surge of relief and felt this peace over me like God was telling me this needs to happen and that everything is okay. Then, on August 21st, my husband unexpectedly showed up at our home. It was the first day of school for the children and he wanted to take them to the bus stop to see them off on their first day. It was about 7 a.m. when the front door opened. The children were so excited to see him that they ran down the stairs, gave him a hug, and jumped in his arms.

As I looked out the window and watched him walk down the street with the children to the bus, I wondered what happened to the man who I married. He gathered around with the other parents chatting, laughing, and talking, with the neighbors not knowing what this man had done to our family, and with the neighbors not knowing that this man was no longer living underneath our roof. He was at the corner gathered with the other parents as if everything was as it had always been, and it was not. After he saw the children off to school, he opened the door and I was in the kitchen washing dishes. This was a surprise to me as I thought he was just going to get in his car, pull out of the driveway, and return to where he had come from, but he did not. He walked into the kitchen, went into the family room, laid on the couch, and we began to talk. He asked how I was doing, and I replied that I was okay. I asked how he was doing and how was work and it was almost as if none of this was really happening. Then, we began to speak about our situation. I had to let him know that I forgave him for what he had done to us and I said it with all of the sincerity that I had in my heart because I still loved him. However, I was in denial that this is who he had become. I told him that I forgive you, I forgive you because I have to, I forgive you because I want to, I forgive you because I love you, and I have to forgive you for me. He just looked at me and said, "I do apologize for letting a friend get this deep into our marriage." I no longer asked what that meant. I took it for what it was. As I said to him early on and the same thing that I said to her was that a friend would not allow a married man to stay in her home, regardless of status. She was not a friend in our marriage, and I knew nothing about her.

After he said that, he admitted that she had come on to him, which was no surprise. I believed it that went both ways. We then started speaking about our separation. He asked what I wanted in the divorce. I told him that I had been looking at some homes since the house was no longer sacred and I did not feel comfortable there. I also told him where these homes were located and asked if he wanted to check them out. He replied that he would, but that it would need to be done at another time and that he would schedule a convenient time. I also told him where the kids would be going to school and we discussed other things that we wanted when we separated. This was all so surreal, as there was no arguing and it sounded as if we were planning a family vacation. Even now, after knowing that it was another woman, I told him that I did not want to take him to court for child support under the conditions that I did expect for him to be responsible where I would not have to ask him for support.

Of course, this did not work down the line, but more will be discussed on this topic a bit later. As I was sitting there looking into the eyes of my husband, I just could not help but to have those feelings that were still in my heart for him. He looked at me and we actually made love, which is crazy... I know. What was even crazier is even after that he was still convinced that he had to go. You would have thought that something was after him the way that he left the house. The next day, August 22nd, which is our daughter's birthday, we

94

had split visitation. He was scheduled to have her during the day and to return her at 8 p.m. Eight o'clock came and she walked through the door, although he was not with her. When I look at his car was driving down the street, it was such a sad time for me. I felt horrible for the kids because we had always celebrated all of our family occasions together, and the man that I once knew would have walked through that door and celebrated our daughter's birthday with us together as a family. I had a cake for her in the kitchen on the table, some gifts, and proceeded to sing happy birthday. It was just me, her, and my son. I know that had to be a hurting moment for them even if they didn't show it because dad was not there with us. It was not the way that it had always been for every moment of their lives for as long as they could remember.

It is now Saturday, August 23rd, and the doorbell rang. I was on the phone with my mother-in-law and placed her on hold as I opened the door. I was then faced by the County Sheriff's office and had no idea about what was going on. I was being served. But, wait. Not only was I being served, I was being forced to be removed from our home with my children. I had no idea what on earth was going on until the police officer told me that Tcee James had a peace order against me. I really couldn't believe this was going on. I mean just 2 days ago, my husband came home and we made this passionate love. Then, the next day he returns, drops our daughter off, then Saturday I'm being served by his mistress. What really baffled me was the fact that I had not seen her since August 1st. I had no idea that any of this was coming, as I had never texted nor spoken with her on her phone even though I had her phone number. I never called her even once since August 1st when we parted ways, and to top it all off, this woman hugged me. Now I was being served with a peace order, which was ridiculous and all on account of my husband. All this time I was on the phone with my mother-in-law, who just couldn't believe what was taking place on the other end of the phone. When the police officer told me that I had to gather my things and my children and we had to leave our home until the final hearing, I was baffled. Where was I to go? What was I to do? What was going on with this man? My mother-in-law, who couldn't believe what was going on, told me to come over to her home. So, we gathered some clothes and slept on her couch in her one-bedroom apartment in the living room, on a sofa bed for approximately 1 week until returning for the hearing.

I showed up to court that Monday and there she was. As I entered the courthouse, we didn't say anything to one another. Shortly after the court was open for us to walk in and have a seat, the judge called our names. I explained to the judge that I had no idea why I was even there, and that nothing had transpired between this woman and me. I further explained that I was served and two days later had to appear without any witnesses or preparation for a matter that I knew nothing about or shall I say that I thought was already resolved. I asked the judge if this case could this be postponed so that I could have time to bring in my witness, and the judge granted my request. One week later when we returned, as I was driving towards the courthouse to park, I noticed my husband's car drive by me when I saw the gold Masonic emblem on the back of his car. In disbelief, I was thinking to myself what is this man doing? As I pulled in and parked, my girlfriend had just arrived to testify and I mentioned to her about seeing my husband's vehicle. This entire ordeal had been a sad occasion for those who admired the marriage that we once had and looked up to us as the model marriage to emulate. This truly broke her heart that we were going through this. As I entered the courthouse again, this time with my witness and I sat down, my husband walked in shortly after and we spoke. He said, "Hello," and I responded. Then I asked him if we could speak in private. We went behind the door near the elevator and I asked him in a soft voice why was he here, and he carried on as if he did not really understand why he was there. He told me that Tcee had requested that he come, but he really did not say one way or the other the real reason why he was there.

All I could say to him was, "No matter what we are going through, I am still your wife and there are certain things that you just do not do. It is my hope that you are not here to testify against me because I would never ever do that to you no matter what. I am still your wife, you are still my husband and it is our income that feeds those kids mouths. I don't know what's going on between you and her. This is your stuff that I got dragged into because you were dishonest with me and I just hope that you own up to that and realize that we don't deserve this." Once I said those words, I returned to the waiting area. As I was sitting there with my girlfriend, my husband's new side chick had to be seen. She let me know that she was in the picture now by using profanity to try to provoke me to respond as she was speaking to the women who were next to her. These women were present on August 1st during the incident. She called me out of my name as she was speaking to them using the "B" word. Then, she stood up, walked over to my husband, and purposely put her back to me closing me off from their conversation. I was just waiting to exhale, thinking, "Lord let this day be over and let it be over without me going to jail." I did not have time for this woman who clearly did not have any respect for herself, my husband, nor our family. As we were directed to come into the court, it all went down.

As we entered the court, we sat and waited for the judge to call us up. Then, when a different judge from the first appearance by the way called us up I took the defendant's side and Tcee took the plaintiff's side. She started her case with announcing herself as Major Tcee James, who has served in the Army for approximately 26 years, and the fact that she and my husband have been friends for 30 years, that they had nothing going on, and that me, Mrs. Jones, was accusing her of having an affair with my husband, Mr. Jones. She further went on to say that on August 1st, I tried to break in her front door, which was a complete lie and utterly false. What actually happened? The thing that hurt the most was that I received the answer that I had asked my husband about in the hallway prior to us entering the courtroom regarding him testifying against me. When the judge asked whether she had any witnesses, the two women and the other guy who were present on August 1st were not the only ones who stood up in Tcee's defense. My husband also stood up, walked with them to the front of the courtroom, and sat on the side waiting to be questioned.

Therefore, I was able to cross-examine Tcee and ask her about the events leading up to the events that took place on August 1st and leading up to August 1st. I asked if she allowed my husband to sleep in her home, and she replied, "Yes, he had been spending the night at her house." I then asked about August 1st when I came back to return his things. She bravely denied the fact that we had this conversation outside and that she hugged me when I asked about this event. I was so shocked that I almost couldn't continue the questioning because it was evident that they were up to something. They were up to no good, and the part that was really unbelievable for me was when I cross-examined my own husband on the stand. Prior to my cross-examination of my husband, I had the feeling that this hearing was really not going to be fair. First, because my husband turned completely against me as his wife, when I was involved in his mess, not mine. Second, the fact that everyone on the other side of the table was clearly not being honest about the events that had taken place, I knew that I had a challenge stacked against me. I was standing there with my integrity, being the person that I know I am, being honest, and owning the fact that, yes, I did show up to her home, but nothing else that she was claiming that happened actually occurred. She was leaving out so many facts that would support my case and what did actually happen.

When I cross-examined my husband, I asked him whether he had been staying nights at Tcee's home and he said, "Yes." I then asked him whether he recalled telling me that Tcee told him that she hugged me. He said, "No." By this time, I was completely in disbelief that any of this was even happening. Then, it was Tcee's turn to cross-examine my husband. I could clearly tell that they had rehearsed and exactly how they were going to play this day out.

As the song says, "When you've done all that you could, you just stand." At that point, I knew that the enemy was present and that all I could do was just stay in. Every one of her witnesses who took the stand was dishonest about what occurred that evening. Then I took the stand and was cross-examined by Tcee. It was just an awful day. Everything that I presented and all of the evidence that I showed, everything that I proved at the end of the day, the judge looked at Tcee and said, "Ms. James, I believe your testimony. Mam, I believe that there is nothing going on between you and Mr. Jones." Then the judge looked at me and she called me tacky. I remember so clearly... just smiling because that's all I could do. I just had to smile and say, "OK." I nodded my head, took a seat, and the peace order was granted for Tcee. I just had to take this hit as hard as it was and as much as it hurt to see my husband go against me, the man who I loved unconditionally. After a decade of sharing my life with him, he turned on me and on his family for a woman who is supposed to be his friend? Excuse me, but no friend is going to allow you to do that to your family. No friend is going to aid you in doing that to your family. No friend that respects you is going to allow you to do that to your family, period.

As far as I was concerned, she was never considered a friend to me, and my husband was not the man who I thought I had married. So, what are we dealing with here? We're dealing with rejection and deception. How do you handle that? How do you handle when you've been blindsided thinking one thing and all along it's not what you thought it was? How do you handle when it's all revealed and it's your reality? It's what you are faced with and it's a life-changing situation. How do you handle that? Well for me, I remained present. As difficult as it may sound going through such a crisis, the more I remained fully present in what I was dealing with, I was not in denial of anything but vested fully in it. It was then that I was able to clearly accept it and clearly see a way to keep peace in my life so that I could handle what I was faced with. When you're busy trying to ignore what really is your reality, you're not dealing with the pain, you're not dealing with the anguish, and you're not dealing with the adversity. When it's not being dealt with, it's not being resolved. No matter how bad something hurts, no matter how much energy it draws out of you to face it, really that's the best solution. The only way to come out of it, is to face it head on. Some of the ways that I was able to deal with this was to keep myself active and to help others. I truly believe that you're helping yourself when you help others, which in turn helps you keep a good spirit and you can deal better with the things that are going on in your life. I remain grounded in my spiritual life physically and emotionally, having found tremendous reward in helping others navigate through their adversity. Once I realized that the way I was handling my crisis was something that most women would not be able to bounce back from, I knew that I had to share my story with others. I wanted to let them know that they could realize that they do not have to be a victim of their circumstances, which can serve as opportunities to grow and to take on a new lease on life, which is actually what it did for me.

When we separated, there were things that I knew I had to be able to do no matter what. I had to be in the right mindset because I had two children who I had to take care of no matter what. I had to be in the right mindset so that I could work and provide for them no matter what. So, when you're faced with that, you make the decision to fall apart or pick yourself up, keep your head high, and stay keep it moving. Period. And, as horrible as this situation may seem, I experienced an indescribable peace that I knew was a peace from God and a peace that I knew that I would be okay, a peace that I knew that it was already taking care of. Today I live a life of gratitude and I live a life of thankfulness. I'm thankful for the time that I did have with my husband because I truly believe that everyone is put in your life for a reason and once their reason has been fulfilled there has to be a way for it to end because it wasn't always meant to last. We don't know the story of our lives, but each of us has one already written. So when crises occur, it's not meant for us at that moment right away to understand why. You can think I thought I was this and I thought I was that, and that I love this person who I thought loved me, and all of those things can be true. However, when it's not in your blueprint for something to last, our role has already been fulfilled and it has to end. We don't choose that ending necessarily all of the time, but when it has to end it will end. Therefore, I'm not bitter and appreciate what we had. I'm really excited about the future and, in fact, hope that my husband finds true happiness again. If it's with her, I hope that they live happily ever after or until their season is over. There is no need for me to be in the "Bitter Women's Club" because I have so much to be thankful for.

There is so much more life in me to live for. If nothing else, always remember that all relationships have a purpose and a meaning. Even if they were relationships that didn't turn out quite the way that you expected or relationships that you felt were toxic, each relationship has a purpose to teach you something or provide you with something from which to grow. For that, be thankful. The amazing part of this story for me is how you can be under the impression that life is settled and that all is well from one day and then the next one. Then, all of a sudden, you're trying to put back the pieces to a broken puzzle. My husband has said to me that if anyone ever asked him what happened to us that he would just say that, "We had a good ride." To this day, I still don't know exactly what happened since as I mentioned earlier nothing was ever said to me. He always told me that I've always said that I loved him and that if I loved him enough the way that I said that I do that I would let him go. He also told me that I needed a fresh start. Therefore, the only thing that I can get out of this is like he said it to me in the kitchen on August 21st when he apologized for letting a friend in too deep into our relationship. I believe it went further than even he expected it to go and was too far-gone as he also stated to me to return. And, that's okay because I know that I tried everything in my power not to give up even when he was wrong. Wanting to keep my family together and wanting to forgive him and us to work this out was what I wanted to do and was everything that he did not want to do. With that said, that is a part of the peace that I have because I know that I tried everything to keep my family together, and I have *no regrets* because of it.

I will forgive those who have harmed me in the past and peacefully detach from them, as a river of compassion washes away my anger and replaces it with love.

FORGIVENESS

To forgive, something has to be let go of, and that something is grief. As hard as this may be, when we go through challenges, forgiveness is necessary if we want to move on and if we want to have and live the best lives for ourselves. It's natural to be disappointed because of the actions of others, but at the same time, it is unhealthy to hold onto that disappointment to where it affects how you navigate your life and how you navigate your relationships because of past hurts. I had to realize this with not only my husband, but what I also realized with my mother is that, although I have forgiven her and tried tirelessly to have a relationship with her, it takes two to move forward. When the other person isn't willing, just know that you've done your part in trying to mend those relationships. Today, I'm at the point in my life where I have forgiven her, but it is not necessary for me to have to feel the need to want to have her as a part of my life. I've had people not understand that I'm okay with moving forward, not having that relationship, and mistaking that for me not forgiving. There is a difference with not forgiving someone and with being okay with where you are in your relationship so that you can move forward. I have truly forgiven my mother and even her husband. I have sincerely forgiven him. At the same time, there are boundaries that are present because of the strained relationship.

Sometimes you have to forgive and be okay with the distance, because having the distance is necessary. For me, the distance is necessary in my life regarding my stepfather because this is someone who I will not allow to be around my children, and it is my duty and obligation as their mother to protect them. That has nothing to do with not forgiving. There are just some relationships that need not exist for the best interest of others and in my case, that's exactly what it is with my mother. Maybe one day God will put it on her heart to come around and mend the brokenness, for the sake of herself, for some closure for me, and her relationship with her grandchildren. That is something that I continue to pray about. In the meantime, I respect the distance and do not harbor any hard feelings, even with my husband. Even as disappointed as I was with him being under the impression that he was my soulmate, the head of our household, and our protector, then to learn a decade later things from the family that I never knew about and having to accept how he abandoned us, I have forgiven him. I told him that I forgave him for what he had done because I loved him and also because I had to forgive him for me to move forward. Unfortunately, things aren't the best between us at the moment. My only hope one day is that we will be able to communicate and co-parent in a "healthy way."

It is so easy to be bitter when someone hurts you. However, it's even easier once you forgive someone, as this allows you to move on because after a while bitterness becomes extra energy and effort that you're exhausting, which likely affects no one other than you. Life is so much more pleasant when you have a free heart. What I mean by "free," is a heart that's not imprisoned with hatred and grief. Life will always have its challenges and forgiveness is something that we are always going to have to be faced with because it isn't perfect. Forgive others for you. This is when you can make it about you. Instead of making it about that person who hurt you, make it about yourself and being whole. Know that if you don't forgive him or her for whatever it is, that you're doing yourself a disservice and consequently those who you love a disservice, because whenever you go through something in life it affects those around you that you care for. This is because you're holding on to that anger and it's disguised, and when it does come out, it will surface in other ways. Frequently, you don't even know why you're angry nor why, when things happen, that you don't always handle them in the best manner. It could be all of that anger and debilitating unforgiveness pent up in you and subconsciously you don't even realize that you are letting it affect who you are and your character and then it ends up being who you become. Pray for those people in your life and pray for yourself in the process. When you give it to God, that's all you have to do. Have faith and believe that He's got you. No matter how you feel and who you have or don't have to turn to, you'll always have God.

Please don't allow it to be just about you and how something has made you feel. Think about all of the other people who are affected on your one decision not to forgive. Think about that for a minute. Think about how other people are tied to what we should do in some fashion or form. Have a relationship with that one person who is blocking you or you who's blocking yourself from that one person to forgive. Some instances are rare, such as mine in regards to my stepfather and his relationship with my children. There will be rare occasions where there are people who are simply unhealthy. So, rightfully, you have made a decision to not have them be a part of your life for one reason or the other. When the issue is something that is not detrimental, such as an argument, a misunderstanding and/or a communication gap, for example, try your best to rectify those situations, but do it for you or for the other person. Most important, do it because this is what God would want you to do. He has forgiven all of us and sacrificed and given His only son for our sins. If He could do that, we can certainly forgive others for what they've done to us.

I will honor my feelings and achieve anything that I set my mind to do. I will dissolve and dissipate all anxious, confused, or fearful thoughts, be peaceful in my mind and heart, and in the present moment, I will be poised and centered.

HOW TO FIND POWER WHEN POWERLESS

How do you find the power when you're powerless?
How do you find power when you're experiencing a
crisis? How do you find power when you are going
through a change in your life? You find power by
being still and you find power by accepting your
reality and dealing with it. The most powerful thing
that you can do is to be present in your powerless
moment. Let me repeat that. The most powerful
thing that you can do is to be present in your
powerless moment. I say that because the way in
which you deal with things is by being present, the
way in which you come up with a resolution is by
being present, and the way in which you can
understand and appreciate your moment is by being
present. This is how you become powerful in fact
when you're powerless. It can be one of the most
life-changing times and in a magnificent way. When
I speak for myself, I know that every time I
experienced some type of adversity, admittedly, it
hurts in that moment; but, it also strengthens you

and forces you to really find out who you are inside. As silly as that may sound, and as simplistic as that may be, this truly is what will make you powerful in your powerless moment. When we are hurt, we're so busy feeling pain and crying in a moment of agony that we don't realize that's actually an excellent opportunity to discover how strong we are inside and what lessons can be learned from the experience.

Frequently, a storm is required to receive the blessing. It's simply a test of your faith, what you're made of, how you're going to handle the situation, and whether you'll stand apart from either being a victim or coming out on the other side as victorious. That's the one thing about me. I've always been a rebel and considered myself protected against anything that I've had to go through. You have permission to feel the pain but what you don't have permission to do is to let it bring you down into such a dark space that you remain stuck in that place.

There is a difference between being *present* and being *stuck*. Those who are stuck are pessimistic and don't see the light in the darkness, meaning the opportunity to grow from this. They are the ones who have the "it happened *to* me" attitude; however, I'm the one who has the "this happened *for* me" attitude. This happened for me *to learn something*. This happened for me *to help others*. When you think positively, it shifts everything. Positive thinking shifts what you do, how you do it, your intention, the things that you accept and do not accept around you, and how you deal with things that remain the same. Are you going to succumb or are you going relish from it? It's in those powerless moments when you're still and listen to God that you can actually hear Him speak and absorb what it is that you should be doing or what it is that you can do to help you. You become creative in these moments. For example, when I separated from my husband and I moved away, it was a very trying time. In that moment I accepted that this was going to be difficult period in my life because I had been with this person for 10 years. We raised a family but that is no longer my reality. Therefore, when I was able to accept the fact that my life was changing, I was better able to deal with it and figure out how to adjust and do things that kept me moving forward, kept me grounded, kept me connected to my spirituality, and that kept me connected to my well-being and health. I began to work out and to read more. I would go to the bookstore and I would read books, such as Tony Robbins' *Awaken the Giant Within,* which was one of the first books that I picked up off the bookshelf. I began to build my book collection in a way that I wanted to improve in all areas of my life at that time.

I also began to read on self-care and about procrastination when I knew I wanted to do things, but just didn't possess the commitment. All of this builds power because you empower yourself. As you start to strengthen yourself, grow, and feed your mind positive energy, you are then becoming powerful. However, it can't be done alone. It can't be done with you just sitting there and dwelling in the moment. That's remaining stuck, and we aren't remaining stuck here! We're accepting that we're being present and that this train is moving to the next station. You can't give up. The more you surround yourself with positive energy, the better *you* will be for *you* and for *your family.* In addition, I was mindful of what I watched on television. In fact, I didn't watch a lot of television, but, when I did it was going to be something that nourished my mind, something that uplifted me, and something that taught me a lesson. For example, I watched Super Soul Sunday, a program that I love, on the Oprah Winfrey Network. It feeds me spiritually and intellectually and I can relate and learn lessons from other people who have had similar experiences, even though we don't have the exact same experiences in life as others. Of course, it's all relative in the way that we handle adversity and the mental and physical outcome are all very common.

Therefore, it is not about *what* happened to you. It's about *what are you going to do* about it? How are you going to thrive from this? How are you going to bounce back? Get outdoors, go to the park, get some sunlight or even read a book somewhere other than in your home. Of course, if you have a place in your home that's comfy to you and it's just your special place, that's fantastic! As mentioned earlier, you should also try to become creative and read in other places, as you will be surprised at the additional positive energy and the new perspectives obtained in your new environment. Frequently, I would read at the park in front of a lake where I could just look up and become lost watching the water. Having that quiet time, having that quiet moment, allowing free thoughts to flow through without distractions, and admiring the beauty of the Earth—the more things that you find to do that enhance your happy spirit, the more powerful you become. Then, it becomes effortless because this becomes who you are and what you enjoy. I find joy in going to the park. I find joy in picking up a book that's going to feed my spirit. I find joy in finding new, creative things to do with my children. Find your joy and you will find your power. It's truly the simple things in life that have the greatest impact, and it's the small changes you make that become habits that become a way of life that you become nonnegotiable about giving up today. Today, I am nonnegotiable about the peace I have in my life, and everything that involves who I am determines whether or not it brings peace in my life, which includes relationships with friends and family and the activities and the opportunities that I decide to become involved in. All of these things are nonnegotiable when it comes to my peace and the more peace you have, the more power you have no matter what is going on in your life.

Let me tell you a quick story since the separation with my husband. He has been acting a mess and I really don't like to say it that way, but it is what it is and has been for a long time. I really was in denial because I was stuck in the past of who he *was* and not who he *is*. Therefore, once I accepted that I had to deal with the present and not relish in the past. I became smarter and realized that the things that he was doing were unnecessary and unfair to the children and to me. I needed to own that and stop giving him excuses, stop seeing the person who I thought he was, and accept him for who he is right now in this moment. For example, he would come to court as you know, and tell fabricated stories and one time even took our daughter to go shooting at the gun range without discussing this first with me just to get a reaction. In addition, when I moved out of our home, he removed items from my office, took them to the police station, and told them that I left something in public view that should not have been there. To make a long story short, after I spoke with the police the police agreed with my version of the events and made him return all of my things to our home. He was doing things uncalled for in the moment of transition, right when our family was struggling, experiencing a crisis, and trying to break down my power. His actions made me powerful in how I decided *not to react* to his actions. There are going to be times when people will try to get a reaction out of you, especially when there is some sort of a breakdown in a relationship and in the communication. Inevitably, that person will try to take you out of your element, especially when they see that you are unaffected like I was and as I continue to be today.

It seems like no matter what I do not do, he has continued to taunt me. Therefore, when you realize that this is the person that you're dealing with, be present and don't get stuck in a negative light, react, and end up looking like Boo Boo the fool. It's okay to be present because you have to deal with your reality before you move on. If you don't deal with it now, you will deal with it later in some other fashion or form. Just don't remain stuck and be mindful of *how* you're dealing with it. Most people couldn't understand how I was so full of positive energy when the separation from my husband occurred. However, it was based on my mindset. I knew that I had to be in a position where I was able to care of myself and care for my children. My reality was my reality. Therefore, it was just that the greater part of it all was how I was going to accept that. I remember when we moved that we went to Target and spent $700.00 on new linens, new dishes, and new cookware. We even bought groceries and that actually felt good. There wasn't much of our past that I removed that I took with me and I was truly being given a fresh start.

So, that's one of the ways in which I handled my emotions going through this storm. I did what made me feel good. I was still present and I methodically thought about out how I was going to carry out my day-to-day activities. When you are busy thinking about how you are going to achieve the goals that you set or how you are going to make your next move with whatever it is that you're working on, you will find that you are too busy to deal with anybody's foolishness. That was me. I was clearly too busy to deal with my husband's foolishness. Moreover, when you exude that confidence, that also gives you power and you become powerful. Even in the midst of the storm you are the decision-maker of your outcome and have every right to be powerful when powerless.

Build power by seeing where you want to be. You are present and accept where you are but do not agree with where you want to be. How do you see yourself in the future? When you determine that, you start to create goals, which lead to the fruition of your vision. Things may not be in the best circumstance as they are now. What you do have now is something very powerful and is a vision for your future. Where do you want to be? What is your why? Why do you want to be there? How are you going to get bigger? What does that look like? How are you measuring your goals? How are you getting there? What is your definitive plan for the future? This is being powerful. The thoughts you attract and the energy that you give off are what determine that future. If you think good thoughts and visualize your life how you want your life to look like with all of the things that you want in it, that will make you feel complete. That will also provide you with holistic success, meaning spiritually with family relationships, financially, and as well as with your well-being (health). What plan are you putting together to make your future rich in all of these areas of your life? When you have the framework and begin to work it, you're being powerful, even in the moment when you're powerless.

My relationship is all about me, him, and no one else. I'm not trying to hide it or to keep it a secret, I just like keeping my favorite things all to myself.

KEEP YOUR RELATIONSHIP PRIVATE

There are ups and downs in every relationship that we have in our lives. The most significant relationship that I am speaking about here is the relationship with our significant other. Often when there's a disagreement, we tend to shut off from one another and vent our frustrations outside of our home. This may be with a best friend, a brother, a sister, or even a parent. We do that because we feel that these are safe spaces and people who we can trust. Unfortunately, there are times where it may even be another male or female who our partner does not know about and that's a whole different set of issues when that comes into play. We look at these individuals as safe spaces for obtaining their valued advice, understanding, and often times for validation if it is something that we feel strongly about and there's a disagreement between us and our partner. We desire validation from others. What ends up happening is that we have people in our ear who don't necessarily have the benefit of the entire picture because we only share what we want to share and, therefore, their opinions are often times based on partial information. My perspective on this is to be very careful with what you share and with whom you share it with. Know the reason why you're sharing it and what you want to come of your sharing with these other people.

A few things happen when we take our issues outside of our relationship. People will become judgmental and it can just be over a simple disagreement that you'll eventually get over. However, once you put that negative vibe out there in the universe about the person that you're with, especially to a family member or a best friend, this is the opinion that they form and often times than not it is ingrained and who they see that person to be. That now truly becomes their perceived understanding. No matter how quickly you got over it or how the disagreement wasn't as big as you thought it was, family and friends hold onto things even when you have the ability to move on and to move forward. With that being said, when you already know that they are holding onto these assumptions, the next time something happens and again these are your go-to people who you trust, who you expect to validate your feelings, who support you no matter what, they will just hear negativity again about this person. Frequently, the advice that they give isn't the best advice that you may need to resolve your matters, and when it does this causes friction in the home.

Keep your relationships private. I can speak to this because during my separation when I was very emotional and not understanding what was going on at the time, I didn't realize that I was doing more damage than good by seeking understanding and support from others who didn't necessarily have my or my husband's best interest at heart. Straight up, people just want to know your business when it comes down to it, whether it's family, friends, or whoever. Not all but most people just want to know what's going on. They'll sound sincere, try to give you advice, and give you the impression that they are being supportive. Be careful with whom you speak and what you speak about. This is especially true if it's a family member or a friend of your partner because 9 times out of 10, no matter how wrong he or she is for what's happening, how they did it, and who they did it with, we all know the cliché that "blood is thicker than water." It doesn't necessarily have to be right or wrong. People make the right decision based on the simple fact that it's family. Now I will give credit to a couple of family members and friends of my husband who realized that what he was doing was wrong. No matter what pain they experienced, they based their opinions on facts and not just because we're family. Those are the people who I respect and that is who I am. Whether with family or not, friends or not, my perception is always based on the facts, which is how it should be. I know it's very difficult when you're upset and don't think clearly about your actions. You become defensive when things are said that you know were untrue, feel that you have to defend your character, and who you are. What I learned is that it's best to be silent, focus on the present, and how to move forward in peace.

As long as you continue to try to defend who you are and try to make people accept and understand you, that will never happen if they already feel that they don't want to. Period. Regardless of what you say or do or what you prove or don't prove, people are going to feel what they feel. Some people are just not going to like you. I will put it out there like that. Some people are just not going to like you, no matter what, which means that it's not about the facts, it's about them at that point, so no justification will change that. That's a personal thing. No justification will change this type of person's feelings towards you. When you're faced with a circumstance where you feel that you're emotionally all over the place, be still so that you can gather your thoughts in a rational way. Don't engage in the e-mailing, texting, and sharing of so-called evidence because it will be used against you. Take it from me. I felt that I had to prove to others what was really going on in my home, so that

135

they could understand what the truth really was. It was a lesson learned and something that I know not to do again. That's with any relationship. Be careful how you include people on the outside. It's best to keep your relationship private. We see evidence of this everyday in the media with celebrities when only one item is leaked. That's all it really takes to get out to some person who wants to make a spectacle of whoever it is. Then, everybody has a different opinion and something different to say. A lot of it may not be true and whatever it is that people want to say will be to their own advantage. So, be careful who you talk to and what you talk about and know that even though your intentions are good that it may be for support or it may be to prove something.

My advice is to just not do it, as you may likely end up on the short end of the stick. You do not owe anybody any explanation for anything about what's going on in your relationship. Any explanation that should be going on should be between you and your partner. That's it. If they are speaking to you and they are the ones that are fabricating a lie, then let them do it. Don't run behind them and try to pick up every little crumb that they drop trying to clean it up. You'll run up hard against a brick wall. In addition, doing so will give you more stress than necessary. Keep the communication between the two of you and if it does have to go outside of the relationship, seek assistance from a professional, neutral party who may be a pastor, Deacon, Deaconess, marriage counselor, or therapist. Any one of these people are best to seek out when you have to discuss private matters outside of the home. These people are trained to ask the right questions, to give the appropriate responses, and don't have an emotional attachment to either one of you. Keep your relationship private. When you do this, you have a greater chance of surviving the storm because you don't have people in your ear who may have hidden agendas. You also don't have people in your ear whose responses are based off of their own frustrations or on just a part of the story that you're giving because they don't know the whole truth. When you keep your relationship private, you have a better chance of surviving the tough times.

Marriage does not guarantee that you will be together forever. I will always remember that I deserve fulfilling, nurturing relationships, and that I'm deserving of love, trust, and kindness. The life in front of you is far more important than life behind you!

LOVE AND MARRIAGE

There is a misconception of what happily ever after looks like. As women, we are excited to be asked the big question, "Will you marry me?" It is something that every woman dreams of, as she matures into adulthood. We see the big, beautiful white wedding dress and all of the beautiful bridesmaids in all of the festivities that are surrounded by this celebration, including the cake and of course the ring. What does all of this mean though when the celebration is over and all of the presents are open, the beautiful reception has closed down for the night and you begin your lives as husband and wife? That is the beginning of a true journey that will tell who you are, what you are made of, and how you will survive and thrive in marriage. Sometimes, people tend to avoid marriage because they figure it's "just a piece of paper" and what's the difference with me staying together with my partner versus getting married and having the relationship documented legally on paper. There is a huge difference! You are biblically and spiritually connected by a vow that you made before God and legally bound by a contract that you made in your state or jurisdiction. Admittedly, a lot comes with this territory and many people don't understand that marriage consists of more than the beautiful wedding dress and cake. It's more than the ring. It's more than a celebration. Marriage is who you are now and who you are made of when you are now living with a person who may come from a different background who was brought up differently than you. You may have values that were never discussed before you decided to get married that now are different than the other person.

How do you agree on raising your children if you have a blended family? How do you work out the finances? Will you have a joint bank account? Will you have separate accounts? When will you discuss your finances? How is that person financially responsible? What is their financial history? These are just some of the topics that we rarely consider until we get married, and I myself had some challenges in these very areas. Some of the mistakes that people make is not having the conversation. First, we assume that all is well because all is well on the surface. What about underneath the surface? When we are wined and dined, told I love you, and showered with gifts, other conversations don't necessarily tell us who this person is. On a more partnership level, however, it does just let me know that they have a good heart or are fun to be around. Having a good heart and being a fun person are not enough to sustain a marriage. Anyone can be funny, have a good heart, take you out, and treat you like a queen. But, a lot more that comes with that package, including taking care of me mentally, emotionally, financially, and having a spiritual link between us. So it's not just what's on the surface, it's also what's underneath that surface. One of the things that I found extremely challenging in my marriage was communication. When it came to our children or the finances and as much as we loved one another, these particular conversations were difficult to have.

These are some of the many things that need to be considered when you're thinking about marriage.

Some of the other mistakes that people make when they get married is that they stop courting. That was another issue in my marriage. Before my husband and I were married, he would plan different outings or we would just enjoy each other's time alone. Once we got married, however, that changed because we moved into our dream home and my husband had to travel a long distance to his job, which gave us less family time in the evening. It was something that we all sacrificed. To make that up I would try to plan things for us to do, such as go on trips with the children as well as without the children, because that was just a part of me and something that I love to do. He would send flowers to my job and on occasion to me at home, which was fine. However, when you stop doing the things that show your intimacy, this is when the relationship can lose its luster. When you're married, have children, and work, we allow our jobs or stress at home with the kids or stress at work with our coworkers and superiors bring us down, and that energy transfers through our relationship with our spouse because he or she is the closest person to us. Many times we do not realize the issues are external factors that we allow to control who we are to one another and how we treat one another. Another mistake is that we don't check in with our significant other, asking questions such as, "Is there anything that I can do to be a better mate for you"? or "What are the things that I am doing that you find work for you, because I want to continue to do those things"?

Frequently, we assume that what we are doing is enough or we take for granted that there could be things that we could do better or that we aren't doing at all. Since the other person isn't saying anything, then I must be doing okay. What isn't realized here is that frequently people keep these things internally and aren't expressive. This can occur at times because they don't want to create any tension or engage in an argument. Depending on the person that you're dealing with, some people can take criticism and others simply can't. To grow in your relationship, however, there will be some things that you are going to be told that you're not going to want to hear. It's just that plain and simple. Not everything is going to be roses and the things that you don't want to hear are frequently the things that you need to hear. Let the feedback sting a little bit, but be intentional about fixing it. The problem was brought to your attention because the issue is a concern, and when problems aren't addressed, as we know, they develop into bigger problems. Be open to having conversations and be open to checking in.

Another mistake that people make is having expectations that their partner is a mind reader. This can actually tie in with checking in because you may hear some things that you assumed were okay or your partner may not know what it is that you really want because you aren't expressive about it. Most times we do what we feel that other person needs and that may not be always the case. They may have some other but we just don't get it because we aren't mind readers. It's not that we don't want to provide those needs; however, if we don't know what they are, what can we provide? How can we provide? If we aren't providing those needs, it is assumed that we don't care or that we're slipping. Effective communication is one of the most underutilized tools that we have available in a relationship and is one of the most important words in the English vocabulary in Webster's dictionary to date! Everything involves communication. How you communicate and why you communicate is essential since no one is a mind reader. We're all human, we all have needs, and we all should be expressive of what those needs are, as well as be courteous enough to ask others what their needs are. When you're in a relationship, it is a constant responsibility to have consideration for the other person. It doesn't end the day that you sign the paper. In fact, it increases the day that you signed the paper because now you are going into a partnership, a real partnership with this person where you both of you are going to be making lifelong decisions together that will impact you, your relationship, your family, and who you are as a couple. Therefore, if you're not communicating or even having those tough conversations, be prepared to be a part of the 50% of failed marriages.

Now I am not saying this from a negative perspective. I am saying this from a real perspective that marriage does work, but you have to put in the work to make it work and the work isn't always going to be pleasant and pain-free. What is pleasurable is knowing that you can have those conversations with someone and that he or she won't take it to heart in a negative way. That you can have conversations about your finances and be on the same page with someone who gets it and knows that it is for your good and for the good of the family is a wonderful thing. Here's an example of what that looks like. Have you ever seen that couple who is celebrating their 50th wedding anniversary and their love for one another is so admirable to you? Some people even wonder how did they do it? I guarantee you that they would tell you that they've always dated, always respected one another, and met each other in the middle. They will also tell you that they had those difficult conversations but ended them with respect and the understanding that we want to be here together no matter what, until death do we part, and that we will do whatever it takes to make it work even when it's difficult. You have to be willing to love that other person, even when it is difficult to love them. I've been there. I know what that's like. Heck, I'm there now and we aren't even together. When you can love somebody, even when they are being difficult to love, they can't get any better of a person to be by their side because at that time you are illustrating that it's not about you. It's about us. Yes, I don't like you right now. I don't like what you said. I don't like what you did. Whatever the case may be, however, my actions are letting you know that I do still love you. And, with the words that I say and how I communicate with you, you know that I still love you.

When you master that, you are on the right track to having a very successful relationship. Now this is not to say that your relationship may not end in the future. Some relationships end and they become complete because they went as long as they were supposed to. Yes, I do believe til death do we part, because no one (at least I believe no one) gets married to get divorced. We all have intentions of forever-lasting futures when we take that next big step. Sometimes things happen in life because people have to be removed for reasons that you don't understand at that time, because they aren't your reasons, or may not even be your decision. It is just so. Therefore, just be reminded that you must communicate with full transparency if you want to have success in your marriage or relationship and that is the only way that you can be completely and fully understood. Fully transparent equals being fully understood or even if not fully understood, because sometimes people take understood as agreeing. You're not going to always agree, but at least I know what you're thinking. If I don't know what you're thinking, then my reactions may be different. My actions may not meet up to your

149

"expectations" and we'll both fall short. So be mindful the next time you are feeling a certain way and ask yourself what have I done to make myself clear. Is there any way that I could have prevented the way that I'm feeling? Maybe it's me. Maybe it's my lack of communication. Or, if it is the other person, sit down, have a conversation, and figure it out. When we have conversations, frequently we need to be able to compromise so that we can to the best of our ability, have understanding. What do I mean by this? When we're having a conversation, and it's one of those conversations that are difficult to discuss, we're quick to want to respond instead of listening. It becomes an emotional roller coaster and leads to a disaster. We want to be defensive about every point that we hear and feel that is not right with our soul, and that it just isn't resonating with us. Sometimes, we just have to let that be known.

My confidence, self-esteem, and inner wisdom are increasing with each day; I will pay close attention to what my mind, body, and soul need for health and vitality.

SHOW UP, EVEN WHEN YOU DON'T FEEL LIKE IT

Personal Care

There have been many instances where I could have fallen apart and simply given up. However, that was not, and remains to date not to be a viable option for me. There will be days where you're drained, especially if you're a single mom raising not only one child but multiple children and having to tend to their needs every day, in addition to your own. Your days can be draining, and when you're going through a crisis there may be times when you don't even feel like getting out of bed because you just don't have the energy to do so. It's all about mindset and the things that you do, like showing up, is what matters. You have to show up even when you don't feel like it. Even when you don't feel like it, get out of bed. Make up your bed. Something that simple can jumpstart your day. Don't leave your bed messy, as a messy room will let your house fall apart and that's only going to make you feel worse. That's visual clutter, which then leads to emotional clutter, which then leads to internal clutter. By then you're so far out of whack and don't even realize why, it's like letting the dominoes fall, one action affects the other. So personal care is one thing that is really important when you're going through a situation where life has changed or there has been a loss, in which grieving is normal. When you get up, what does your self-talk look like? This is all a part of personal care. What positive energy are you feeding yourself? Who do you see when you look in the mirror? Who are you representing when you walk out the door? Your outside does not have to be a mirror of your inside. However, your outside also attracts to you what you appear to be on the outside. Therefore, especially during times like this, you want to attract meaningful relationships with people who can pour into you and spread their positive wisdom. I believe that who you were before your circumstance should be magnified 10 times during your transitional period.

If you kept your hair done before your circumstance, continue to keep your hair done. If you were always a nice dresser and treated yourself well, continue to do that, as your personal care is important to your self-esteem, in your confidence, how you exude who you are to the world, and how you show up in other areas of your life. Frankly, if you look a mess, you're going to feel a mess, especially if that's not the person that you're used to being. Now granted, things may change especially when you're going through a divorce as far as money is concerned, but there are ways around that. As I tell my children there is more than one way to skin a cat, and there is no excuse to not take care of yourself. Taking care of yourself and of your personal care is another part of that being powerful when powerless. Don't you feel good when you get a new dress or some new shoes? When you get your nails done, it feels good, right? Then, why not do that and why not make a means to do that? It doesn't mean for you to go out here and blow $1K in clothes and accessories without considering your finances. During this time, it does mean that you need to be conscious of the things you're letting go when it comes to you and who you are.

Personal care doesn't always require money. Personal care could be taking a time out for yourself. Something I highly recommend that each one of you do is to take a time out, a time to reflect, a time to breathe and continue to discover who you are in this process. This requires time with you and only you alone. That is also a part of personal care. If you are continuously pouring into others, such as your children or your extended family or tending to whatever the circumstance that is happening in your life at this time, you're taking away from your personal care. Your personal care should come first above everything, because in order for you to be able to be that mom or pour into others, you have to be everything to yourself first. You can't pour everything if your glass is half-empty, so personal-care is essential. It's one of those necessities that's *no matter what.* Have you ever experienced that no matter what? I will continue to do this no matter what. I'm going to achieve that no matter what. This is going to be my goal this year and I'm going to be successful at it. No matter what, I am going to take charge and honor my personal care.

For Your Children

Although you may not feel like it, you also have to continue to show up for your children. Your children are watching you and seeing how you handle things, as the way in which you address and resolve issues is what they will likely inherit unconsciously. So please be mindful, as children are little sponges and they absorb *everything* that they hear and are much smarter than we give them credit for. Showing up is the most powerful way to show your children that there will be rainy days. However, the way in which you show up will determine how you come out on the other side. Show your children that in the midst of the storm that we're still able to be thankful. That's one of the things that I've been able to do, continuously point out the things that they should be thankful for, including the things that God is providing for us even in the storm.

As stated before, when the children have days out of school, we volunteer for community service events. I've had them assist with food drives for those who are less fortunate because I want them to see that helping others helps you as well, which it does. Another way of showing up is being powerful when powerless, right? It also shows the children that there are less fortunate people who don't even have what you have, since they have to visit a food bank to receive goods and are unable to buy groceries at the grocery store, which so many of us take for granted. Therefore, please be mindful when you're going through your circumstance, and continue to show up for your children. Magnify that 10 times and show up at your children's schools to show that even though we are a single-family, single-parent family household now that you still have the support of your parent, which has not waivered and is not going to change. If anything, it's going to show up more powerful than it had in the past because I know you need to be more present than ever before. I would drop in on my kids at school for lunch and bring them pizza or if their performance was noteworthy and they received an excellent grade on an exam or on their report card, I would show up early, get them out of school, and take them to the park. Again, these actions that you are doing to help others is helping your happy spirit, which is helping you become more powerful when powerless. This all ties together.

The next time you experience a backwards turn in life or if you're currently experiencing one now and you're a parent, remember that your children are innocent and that it would be unfair for them to experience what you're going through. Show up for them, even when you don't feel like it. Put on your Broadway actress skills. That doesn't mean that you aren't owning your reality and it doesn't mean that you aren't being present. It simply means that you're showing up and that you are demonstrating to your children that there is ample opportunity to change any situation, to do better, to be better, and to move forward.

On the Job

If you're experiencing trouble at home and go into the office, more likely than not, your troubles follow you and there is no separation between work and home. You have to show up even when you don't feel like it because you know that you have bills to be paid, you know that you have mouths to feed, and you know that your job is your source for that to happen.

I'm speaking from experience here because when I separated from my husband, it was very difficult for me to work. I could not focus because I was trying to understand what was going on, as well as make strategic decisions on where we were going from here as far as the children were concerned. I literally could not function for a little over a month. I wasn't showing up the way that I used to, and I wasn't performing at the exceptional rate that I once had. My professional position was being affected by my circumstance, and looking back, I realize that not only should I have shown up physically when I did not want to, but that I should have shown up through my performance when I did not want to. It is a difficult time, certainly I get it. I am not talking bluff here.

However, your circumstances must not interfere with your coins. This is important for many reasons. First, you don't want your drama written all over your face. When I say that, I mean that you do not want to look like you're going through something. Your employer may not know what you're going through, but they know what they see and you can look disinterested, as if you don't want to be there, which you really don't and mentally you're not. Second, you may have not shared what you're going through with your colleagues or your boss. I would even be conscious of sharing too much information because people do judge, but your job is another place where you are definitely going to have to provide that superb grand-standing performance. People will always remember the negative before they remember the positive. So, when you go on the job show up no matter what. Look your very best. Don't go to work looking like you're going through something. You can deal with that when you get home. One day when you look back on all of this, you will see the things that you could have done better or you will be proud of the things that you did come through in the way that you did. No matter what, show up even when you do not feel like it!

Happiness is my birthright and I will embrace it as my set point state of being!

HAPPINESS

Happiness is a personal journey, and a quest that one has to take for herself or himself to fully understand what having true happiness means. We frequently rely on others to complete our feeling of happiness when we enter relationships not realizing that we should already be happy and that those relationships only further nurture what we already have that resides within us. What does happiness look like? That's only a question that *you* can answer. Before you respond, you must fully understand what it takes for you to be happy without relying on someone else to accomplish that task for you.

I'll help you out here. Happiness comes from the feeling we receive from things that we do as individuals for ourselves or even for others. This provides total fulfillment inside, which in turn, makes us happier people. Happiness does not come from the expectations that we place on others to return to us. Although we don't realize it, when we

163

think that way, we're not only exercising control of ourselves, but essentially we are attempting to control the actions of others. With that said, there will always be disappointment because we are who we are as individuals, and I had to learn this through my divorce. When my husband told me that he loved me but that he just wasn't happy and felt that we had grown a part. Initially, I felt like I was responsible for his happiness. It wasn't until I realized that I'm really not, that happiness is a personal quest, that I released myself from that conviction. So, not only am I going through the process of the divorce of my husband, but I'm being still and taking time to myself through the process, allowing time "to divorce" all of the negative assumptions that I had about who I was supposed to be. This goes back to where I mentioned that many of us enter relationships broken and with unresolved issues not even realizing that although we're with someone new, we're having fun, and things are going great, that it's all an illusion. Because any issues that we had were unresolved and are just that—unresolved. They will resurface and don't necessarily have to do with the other person. When you are feeling unhappy, it could very well have to do with all of the things that you never dealt with in your life. You don't understand why you are short tempered. You don't understand why things trigger a reaction inside of you. All of this is important. That's why you need to take time when relationships are complete to discover, dissect, and understand who you are. It's not only fair to you but it's the fair thing to do for that next person who you will one day spend quality time with. Please understand that's a mistake a lot of us make and that I'm guilty of it as well. Every single relationship that I've been in, which I believe adds up to only three, have always been long-term, and I've entered into each one of them broken. In fact, when my husband I met, I had just ended a relationship and my husband was going through the process of divorce. Was our connection really authentic? When we eventually said those words "I love you" and had those feelings of this is the one, were they really legitimate feelings or were they feelings that were covering voids in both of our lives? Were we really setting up an unstable foundation that had underlying problems? Think about that the next time you're ready to walk away or place doubt on others when it comes to your happiness. Remember that happiness is a personal quest and not the responsibility of anyone else other than yourself.

If you have any addictions that aren't good for you and routinely engage in behavior that does not serve you in a positive manner, the habits that you form could also interfere with your happiness. When you continue to do the same thing but desire different results, what is it that you aren't doing? Do you take time out for yourself? Do you conduct self-check-ins where you ask yourself questions so that you can measure your level of self-satisfaction? These are some of the things to think about when speaking about happiness. Always remember that your happiness is all about you.

You're BRAVER than you believe and STRONGER than you seem! Often, out of our greatest rejection comes our greatest direction.

THE RESENTMENT

Although my husband displayed many loving ways, there were also uncertainties that I chose to live with. When we want to be loved and feel love in other areas, we tend to dismiss problems in our relationships not recognizing them fully as problems. Deep down I always felt hidden and not a part of the family dynamic with my husband when it came to my stepson. I felt that was an area in my husband's life where he created this wall, and in doing that he never really understood my point of view or made it comfortable for me to feel as though I was his other parent. It was difficult and became more challenging when he had expectations of me in how he wanted me to behave towards my stepson not understanding that he had a lot to do with nurturing that relationship. As a caring parent entering into a new relationship and having kids, I do understand that you want your children to be protected. In fairness to the new parent in their life and the love that you're supposed to have for that parent, it's imperative for everyone's feelings to be involved and to feel relevant. Unfortunately, this was not the case with us.

As the years went on and my feelings regarding the situation continued to be downplayed, the closeness never matured the way that I wanted it to. The environment was more cordial as opposed to loving. I brought this to my husband's attention and asked him if we could all sit down, speak about the things that we like, and discuss what we need and would love to have from one another as a blended family. Although I requested this family meeting more than once, it never materialized. This caused me to be resentful towards my husband because he wasn't putting in his full effort to make our family environment the best that it could be. My house became segregated. When my stepson would come over for the summer, he would literally stay in his room. I would be gardening or the kids would be playing and my husband would visit my stepson in his room for the most part. That's where they would be together, which was absolutely fine, but they would spend time in there apart from the rest of us and not include the rest of us, which caused a variety of issues and ill feelings. Many times, I felt as though my husband was my stepson's gatekeeper, as if I had to go through him to be approved and to suggest for him to do certain things. When you're in that type of situation, it detracts from the role of spouse and parent. You feel more like just another person who happens to live there, too. It wasn't as though I was a parent who didn't have an enormous amount of love and attention for her family. I took everyone on trips. I very much enjoyed going out, having family barbecues, and having family movie night because it's what I loved to do and it's what families who like, appreciate, and care for one another do. So, I'm sure through the years that resentment has played some significant part in the deterioration of our marriage. Maybe at the time I didn't realize that some of the emotions I was having were stemming from that feeling. My message to you is that if you do have a blended family and you want it to work, everyone needs to be considered, which includes all of the children and the spouses. Yes, your child has another parent in their life, but when you make a commitment and decide to remarry, that other parent also has feelings and should be considered in the process. As needed, consider counseling as a resource for resolution. No one knows everything, and that's one of the things that we need to be willing to understand and then we can avoid such tremendous disappointment. Someone else can help us realize that our expectations may not be reasonable or fair. I do believe that the blended family dynamic can work; however, it takes an "all-in" to make it happen.

One of the other areas of my life during the course of my marriage that harbored much resentment is the decision to abort one of our pregnancies. It was a one-sided decision and a decision that I fought. We were pregnant with twins and I recall the hurt that I felt when my husband expressed that he did not want this pregnancy. Unfortunately, I did have an abortion when I was younger. I was a teen at the time and did not think it was a fit nor appropriate for a married family and as a married woman to be pressured into a situation where I was not allowed to have my children based on the feelings of my husband. I even almost told him that I was willing to walk away from our marriage so that I would not have to get rid of these innocent, precious little souls that did not deserve what was going to happen to them. I reluctantly walked into that surgery clinic saddened with tears, and for my husband to be emotionless really made it a tough, tough experience. It wasn't just a regular doctor's experience for me. I felt that I was disappointing God, I felt that I was disappointing myself, and that these children did not deserve this. I was a married woman and felt that I should not be doing things like this now. We were grown enough to do what it took to make children, and we should have been mature enough to take care of our responsibility.

To this day whenever I see a set of twins, I always wonder what it would have been like.

Allowing someone else to make that decision for me because I wanted to keep a happy home really deteriorated happiness within myself. I really felt like I allowed someone else to let a piece of me die. I asked God for forgiveness because I was so confused. As a wife, I believe in honoring my husband. At the same time, I was so confused that I did not know in honoring my husband whether I was committing a sin and disappointing God. It wasn't even about me. I ignored my hurt and wondered whether I was doing the right thing. When they gave me a pill and told me to take it, that was the beginning of the process. I asked to go to the restroom, and when I closed that door I just cried because I knew there was no turning back. In that moment, I became numb and wanted it to be over. I became robotic. I just allowed everyone to tell me what to do so that I could get out of there. The doctor laid me on the table and that's when I heard this loud machine, like a vacuum, which literally felt like it sucked all of the life out of me because it did. I wasn't even sure how I felt about

my husband after the procedure. I wasn't even sure
how I felt about anything anymore.

The most important vibration to be aware of

is our own!

WHAT ENERGY DO YOU ALLOW?

The energy that you allow in your space is what sets the tone in your day; in who you are and in how you present yourself to others. The one thing that I am very guarded about is the energy that I allow into my space. Negative energy is not an option. We cannot avoid negative energy but we can cast it away when it comes into our presence. Negative energy will always be around but it doesn't have to be accepted and that's what I want you to know. You have control of the energy that you allow in your space. Having peace of mind is a choice and when you choose to allow yourself to get involved with other people who project negative energy upon you, you then become a participant in their frenzy, taking away from your own energy and peace.

The next time that you're confronted with this resistance and you can feel that the quality of that air is contaminated, take a step back and evaluate the situation. You'll see that it's there to knock you off course to get a reaction out of you and to put you in a space that you don't want to be in. In that moment reclaim your power and overcome that negativity. Of course, lighting candles is a favorite of mine, as you already know. These are just some of the things that help me come back to my center because my center and my inner peace are both extremely valuable and important to me. I cannot function in chaotic environments because they are not something that I want to be a part of and I'd rather have calm in my life versus disruption.

Everything boosts in a positive way when you think with a positive mindset, which includes your productivity, reaching your goals, setting healthy relationships with others, and how you communicate. Whatever space you're in determines the outcomes in all of those areas. Be careful about the intentional and unintentional negative energy in your space. No one should own that power except you and it doesn't have to always come from a person. It can generate from the music you listen to, the reality shows that you watch, or the type of literature that you read. Negative energy doesn't have to come from just one source. Anything you listen to, see, or watch all plays in how your day and life are projected. So, please don't take it for granted. The energy that you receive not only sets the tone for now; it sets the tone for your future.

I affirm that I know that I am exactly what

my child needs!

HOW TO SURVIVE SINGLE PARENTING

Create a Supportive Environment

Whenever a household is disrupted, not only does the relationship take a turn, but the emotional stability of any children that are involved is also affected. It is very important to keep in perspective the emotional welfare of your children when relationships end. In my case, being together with my husband for over 10 years, our family had an extremely close bond and our children were never without at least one parent. It was always the both of us at all times, and we did everything together. We had fun vacations and enjoyed family time hanging out at the house just being around each other. Children will miss these things. Initially, the shock of it all doesn't get to that point because they are still trying to understand why things are changing. Eventually when you settle into your new lives everyone starts to reflect, including those who are no longer in that relationship with one another, and you reflect on the good times that you shared.

It is imperative for you to be able to provide a supportive environment for your children, and to be able to create an environment where they're receiving love at home from surrounding family members and friends. Try to keep a routine, and if you have anything that you once had in place as far as structure. I'm very structure oriented, so my children had schedules for everything and I wanted to put things back to normal as much as I could for them. For instance, for years we've always visited the library on Mondays. I would allow them to check out five books for the week. My children loved to read, so they would also have available a weekend comic book. That was something that we did as a family and something that they enjoyed. We always loved parks and to this day, this is where we spend most of our time.

I tried to recreate an environment that was familiar to them although it was a new location because we had left our home. It was still an environment that they were familiar with, being outside playing with other children, riding bikes, skating, and just being kids. I'm known for being the spontaneous mom so of course it didn't end there! We would jump in the car and say, "Hey, let's go ride to the beach!" and we'd take a lovely road trip for the day. That's something that I'd done even when we were together as a family and that I wanted to continue to show the children that life goes on. Yes, we're minus some family now but we've also gained a lot. We've gained more time with one another because I'm definitely more involved with my children now than I've ever been because I am aware that this is all just as new to them as it is to myself. Besides, I'm really all that they have, all that they know, all that they can rely on, and they count on that. So, when you're going through relationship changes, of course it can be difficult for you as the parent, but also remember that the children are affected as well. In addition, be careful how you speak about the other parent around them and what emotions you allow to cloud your judgement. No one said that this was going to be easy, but it is doable. It's a must if you want to create an environment that is conducive of raising your children in the best light possible. The more structure you have, the better it is for you as a parent to operate from day to day and not be all over the place doing things in an aimless fashion. The more structure you have, the more that your children know what to expect from day to day. The more that you provide for them emotionally, the better off they will be as all of you continue to navigate through the process, which leads me to my next subject.

Balance

What is balance? I sometimes get conflicted with the word in the sense that it's used in. Can we really balance our lives? Let's face it, something new is always going to happen. You're always going to evolve into the next thing. There's always going to be a setback. There's always going to be something that happens when you think that your life is "balanced." So, is life ever really balanced? No, it's not.

Management

What we do is manage life especially during times when situations are challenging and you have all of these various changes occurring. How are you going to manage that? How are you going to manage keeping your mind right, your spirit filled, and your soul in the right place? It's important as a family and as a single mom to be able to provide for your children holistically. How are you providing spirituality for them? What are you allowing them to see, to watch, and to hear during these times in which they can be easily influenced when they already feel broken? Are you demonstrating that maybe life is just an illusion that can be easily swayed away?

Yes, it's pressure! This is a time that as a mom that you have to step up. You need to let them know that I'm there no matter what and that I will provide for you know matter what even though it's hard for me right now. You have to manage all of that. When you find that sweet spot—when you feel that this will work, I feel that I'm on a level playing field now, I can do this, the children are okay, and I'm OK—that's when you're managing your circumstances and that's where I want you to be. I don't want you to be broken and having your children suffering from your broken spirit by you being in a broken place. I'm going to need you to be strong now because when you look those babies in their eyes, you need to know that you're going to have to provide for them no matter what—no matter who gives you child support or who doesn't, no matter who shows up to be dad and who doesn't.

You are always going to be mom and don't think that children don't understand. Children are very aware of what's going on and they're watching you. They soak everything in like little sponges and although you may not hear it now, depending on the age of your child, *what you do does affect them.* If you manage yourself and manage them, this will come back to you, one day, somehow, in the form of a "Thank you" or either in the form of an "I wish you were there for me more." You make the decision.

You may have to go without frequently so that you can provide for your children. I'm familiar with that but no matter what if I have to spend my last dime on them, the knowledge I have that I was able to provide for them is fulfilling. Knowing that I'm last doesn't matter and that's a part of gratitude—when you know that you could be doing better but you're not complaining about it. You're happy for what you can do and for what you can provide even if it was just taking them to the park, running around, laughing, and having a good time with the children. That didn't cost me a dime, and that feeling is priceless. This all goes into that word "balance," which I call managing. You're managing your circumstances and there is never going to be a true balance, as we are all human and change will always exist.

We're always going to have to manage our circumstances throughout life even though some issues may be bigger than others, such as divorce.

186

You don't achieve balance after divorce; you manage it. You manage the changes, put them into perspective, make them make sense, and then figure out what is that you're doing. You figure out how to pay the bills and you figure out how to meet those goals on all levels (spiritually, financially, for my children, and for myself) then you manage that. There's always going to be a change in each of those categories and when change comes, look at what you have in front of you and sort it out. Put it into its own space, deal with it separately, figure out how you make it make sense, and manage it.

Dating Tips with Kids

Yes, I know that time has gone by for some of us who do wait, and you feel the "itch" to get out there again. You want to be in a relationship. For some of us, it's because that's the attachment that we're used to. For others it's because some time has gone by, we've healed, and we haven't given up on love. Whether you allow yourself to feel and accept that or not because you're hardened, the problem with this is that frequently we don't approach dating and entering back into relationships thinking about everything and everyone that's involved in the decision. Many women are so thirsty for love that they don't put the children into perspective. The first man that rolls up, has a nice smile, a nice body, smells good, and gives you a compliment is the one that you're ready to entertain a little more deeply than you should. We introduce our children to strangers. Yes, strangers, prematurely before we should. Having nice, white, and bright teeth and good conversation just isn't good enough for you to come over and meet my kids. I'm *their gatekeeper*, and I don't need you to be daddy—at least right now. This is what lust and society do to us by comparing ourselves to our girlfriends in what they have and what we don't. We lose our integrity for a man who we're not even married to and whose last name we may not even know. Let me be frank— some of us give it up too early. I know that I'm stepping on some toes, right now, ladies, but it's a fact. We give in too soon without a valid reason.

When you're single, be careful how you date when you have children. In the same way that a mature woman or mature man won't bring an individual home to meet the family until she or he knows that it's serious, that is the beginning of the consideration that you meet my children. We've all made this mistake before so this is not calling the kettle black. However, this is how you learn. For those of us who haven't experienced this, like when hiring a consultant, you're receiving the learning curve without having to make the bad decision that could cost you and your children dearly and more emotional stress than you're already going through. Save yourself that time and drama. Eventually, you'll get tired of the same repetitive outcome in your relationship. So, if you do meet someone, don't take it so seriously from the beginning. I'm not saying that you shouldn't date. I'm definitely not saying that, but be extremely cautious and keep your children and your dates separate. Don't even mention that mommy went out on a date or the person's name. They shouldn't know any of that until you're serious and that may take from 6 months to 1 year from the time you initially met. Take your time. If you want to change your results, change your approach. You'll know when you've changed the approach because it will feel different—almost be like a diet when you know you're doing the right thing, but damn, I want some cake! That's when you know you're doing the right thing. The right thing doesn't always feel comfortable, but at the end of the day, slow down.

Don't post your new status on Facebook as soon as you meet somebody 1 month later that you're in love. You'll look crazy after 3 months changing your status back to single. Slow down! Just like there's plenty of fish in the sea, there's plenty of that, too! Your children don't need to see you with a different man every 6 months. You play a major part in this, too. You may find out something in month 3 that could have saved you from Year 2. Let me say that again! You may find out something in month 3 that could have saved you from Year 2 if you just slow down. Don't wait for a man to treat you like a queen. Treat yourself like a queen and value who you are. If you don't value who you are, you are going to continue to make the same choices. When you value yourself, you're valuing your children. That's when it comes into play. How much do you really value your kids? It's bigger than you and your feelings and wanting to be in love. Be in love with you and be in love with your children enough that you're protective of them and who is going to be in their life. It's no longer about you. Once that seed was planted, you gave up "about you." Date smart and date like an intelligent woman. Date like a caring mom who isn't selfish and thinking only about her own feelings, but about the impact that her decisions have on her children as well.

The moment you take responsibility for your life is the moment that you can change anything in your life!

RELATIONSHIP SURVIVAL TIPS

Awareness

Awareness is not a term that should be taken lightly and is so deep that it is above everything when it comes to the way in which we communicate in our relationships. We must be fully aware that there's a problem, which is bigger most times than what we think the actual problem is that we're trying to address. Those little things that you argue about in your relationship, they're not the problem. Those are the issues that get to you long after the problem has evolved. Unfortunately, the big problem is overlooked because we aren't aware of it now because we're so busy fussing about the insignificant, smaller things. Be very aware when you notice little shifts that appear different in how you normally communicate. These are very important, and please don't take them lightly because it may mean that there's a deep-seeded issue that is resisting the other person. And they may just not know how to talk about it or choose to keep burying it, which is one of the worst things that you can do because all that does is manifest and grow until you explode—similar to the environment of a pressure cooker. So be aware of the subtle changes and mature enough to sit down and discuss it.

Stay on Topic of the Conversation

This is a biggie right here! Everybody wants to be heard, and we tend to start speaking about one thing and then go on our rant. What does that do? It solves nothing. It takes discipline to be able to speak to the person who you love about something that's maybe not so loveable or for you to be on the receiving end. It takes discipline for you to be mature and respectful enough to listen to what you may not want to hear without going on a tangent or revisiting past issues that are supposedly resolved. That's the quickest way to have your partner shut down, and once this happens, the brick wall is up, and that's who (or rather what) you're talking to. So, it's important to stay on topic about exactly what you want to speak about. It actually might not hurt to write this down to ensure that you stay on topic because I promise you that this is one of the things that can definitely kill your relationship. It may not stop thriving immediately, but these are the things that build up over time and what causes frustration. When you bring up old news, why do you do that? When we talked about that issue 1 year ago, we should have left it there 1 year ago because I'm no longer there, you're no longer there, and we moved past that. We can't move forward if we keep moving backwards and revisiting situations that have already been handled. That has nothing to do with right now or with what we're talking about. It has no part in this conversation. When you forgive someone and/or you come to an understanding about what it is that you're speaking about at that place and time, it should be left there at that place and time because it's unfair to the other person no matter whose side it's coming from to bring up something that supposedly has been resolved. I guarantee that if you if you're married, this is shifting the gears up on your way to the courthouse for a divorce. No one wants to be with anyone who doesn't get that we need to communicate effectively, and a part of this process is me listening to you and vice versa, not just through *your* ears. I want you to listen to me and for me to listen to you with all of me in an unselfish manner and not me just wanting to express how I'm feeling. That type of listening needs to go really deep.

Own Up to Your Responsibility and Learn from Your Mistakes

We all make them, and I know that I've said things that I regret. I own up to those things, and I own up to the fact that, yes, I could have said things differently that could have possibly produced a different outcome. That's yet another area where we fail, is owning up to our mistakes. Everything isn't always wrong with the other person, so let's get that clear right now. I don't care who you are or who you think you are or who that other person is who just doesn't measure up. There've been times when you didn't measure up too, and it's never all one sided. So, take responsibility for your own actions. The only way that you can be fully transparent and be able to heal, change, or make better decisions is when you know when you're wrong. When you don't own that, you're missing the possibility for a better you, for the people around you, and for your partner. We can't change what we don't own up to, we can't change what we refuse to recognize, we can't change what we don't deal with, and you can't change what you don't acknowledge, which is very important.

So, the next time you want to chit chat with your mom, your best friend, or whoever it is about what's going on in your household—which you shouldn't be doing in the first place as previously discussed, but you feel the need for some outside support and to vent—be mindful of yourself as well. When you're speaking to your partner, please don't make it one-sided and be careful of the language that you use because frequently we don't realize that our vocabulary is deemed offensive even when communicating our thoughts. For example, when we say things such as, "You always...." That would put anybody on the defense. Instead of saying "you always" or "you don't this" or "you don't that," change your tone, the words that you select, and how you present them. For example, think about saying something like, "I was wondering if... and What are your thoughts?" That's an excellent way to involve the person and to get them to speak more and be accused less because whether or not you see it, you are indeed accusing him or her of failing you in some shape or form. Instead of accusing someone of failing you, which we know the likelihood of getting something positive out of that is zero, remember to have a *conversation* and not an accusation. #tweetable moment.

I cannot control everything that happens to me; I
can only control the way I respond to what happens.
In response, is my power!

WHAT "THEY" SAY IS NONE OF YOUR BUSINESS

During the transition of the separation in your relationships or in your marriage, frequently it can be tumultuous. In fact, the process can just be heart riveting. I am coming from a genuine place of experience. The one mistake that we make when we are so emotional in this storm is that we take it to other people. I'm unsure why we take it to other people; maybe it's for validation for what we did or for comfort. I'm not sure, but you then have the other person who feels that he or she has to defend him or herself and what they stand for, which was my mistake. Actually, it made me look crazy. Now that I look back at some of the things that I did to defend who I am and what was being said or shared, I really did not have to do it because whatever opinions were drawn from those accusations were really none of my business. My business at the time was to focus on me and my children instead of focusing on what was being said and how I could negate those things that I really had no control over. For example, e-mail can be one of the worst vehicles to use when you are going through a situation like this, as people use e-mail to sabotage others. Initially when I was first introduced to the whole situation, I was sending e-mails to my husband wanting him to realize what he had done and what decision he had made, which I felt was unfair. I did this by sending him e-mails of us as a family, pictures, mentioning the things that we loved to do together, asking him to get some help, and letting him know that I was there for him. Ultimately, those e-mails were used against me. I learned from mutual connections that he sent those emails to friends of his because he wanted to make it seem as though I was begging for him to stay. Then once that had gotten back to me along with some other things that were said, I became defensive and wanted to defend me as a person. So, I went on both an email and text tangent responding when I really did not have to do that.

Who are these people for me to have to prove who I am to them? What role do they play in my life where I'm obligated to defend who I am? Frequently, we make the mistake of putting ourselves out there to be sabotaged. This is certainly an avenue that must be avoided because people can take what they want to take and use it against you especially in court. They can pick and choose what piece of communication that they will use against you for their own good. Of course, the entire story won't be told, only those pieces of information that will work against you. So please be careful of how you react when you are reacting to what other people are saying. In the larger scheme of things, your reaction means absolutely nothing. These people really don't care as much about the situation itself as you think, it's all a moment for them. This is entertainment for most of the people that you're sharing your life with, this is reality TV for them. Ninety-nine percent of these people will not be by your side from steps A through Z, as you go through this life changing process. They're just there for you to unload what you're unloading at that time and for you to entertain them and for them to respond. They may have genuine concern for you but they are not going to be the ones who are there with you through thick and thin and from beginning to end. When you know this about a person who is trying to sabotage you, why would you care about what the people who they are communicating to say? Please don't give them that control. I had to learn this the hard way. Unfortunately, those are the lessons that we need, the hard ones. Instead of focusing on what people are saying, quiet it down, don't respond, and begin to draw yourself a new, blank canvas.

Start over and don't beat yourself up about it. What's done is done. It's in the past. Now is the opportunity to start over, and that's what's great about life. Not everything has to be continuous. You have the power to stop it. You have the power to create a new life for yourself, and this is that opportunity. Instead of reacting to something that you know will not even change your current situation, but could potentially make it worse, why continue to feed it? Don't continue to feed something that has no relevancy to you, your peace, or you moving forward. It's not helping that. It keeps you back, and it keeps you stuck. It keeps you back in that space, and isn't that what we're trying to move on from? Why am I sitting here going back and forth with someone who doesn't even matter? What am I trying to prove to this person? And, why? It may be legitimate that you don't want yourself to look like the bad person here. But so what? What is it going to do to you? That's their business what they think. You know who you are and you know whose you are. That's all that needs to be said. When you know that everything else is not relevant. It doesn't matter to me that you talk to your family about me and that you conjure up lies. It doesn't matter to me that you're doing things to provoke a reaction out of me. I will continue to let you do that and keep myself going in the other direction. Because this new life and this new canvas that I created for myself have no room for you. You have to be intentional about what you want. In the process of moving forward, you can't say that you want to move forward and continue having actions that pull you backwards. That keeps you in a negative space because this is what happens when you do that. You're either lying to yourself or you don't have the confidence or the tools and capability to be able to move forward and not feed into those negative situations.

Repeat after me, "What they say is none of my business." It's really not. Why is it none of your business? Because you choose for it to not be. Yes, you have a choice. You get to choose what you entertain. In addition, what you entertain is a deciding factor not only on the outcome but also on how you move forward. The next time you're in a situation, it doesn't even have to be from an intimate perspective, as this could apply to anybody and to any situation. When someone says something about you that isn't true, which we know most times is to cover their own faults, think about the source then think about whether this really is worth entertaining. Think about the vows you made to yourself about wanting peace. Am I serving myself through entertaining this when I say I want peace in my life? If the response is no, well why am I doing it? I know this is nothing but resistance. Why am I allowing it to have an effect on me in this way? I truly need to understand that *what* they say is none of my business, and that I'm not the creator of it, and, therefore, it's not my business. Yes, I get to choose to not be a part of it, and the more intentional I become on not being a part of it, the better life I will live. Period.

Greatness is a lot of small things done well each and every day!

THE BIG BOUNCE BACK!

We have all experienced these types of trials, tribulations, and challenges in our lives. Once the dust has settled and you've shaken off the residue, get ready for *your* resurrection!

Find Your Riches: Rediscovering Who You Are

Frequently, we discover riches in the dark seasons of our lives. It's when we're forced by our circumstances to look at who we are on the inside and what our situations are that we're accepting of and begin to dissect our realities. It wasn't until I was faced with the reality of divorce that I sat still with God and when I realized that I didn't even know who I was. I was confused about my identity—Who am I now? After some time had passed, I realized that God doesn't shut one door without opening another that is more fulfilling than anything I have ever experienced before.

This all comes from my truth and what I live and experience today. Since the separation, I've been put in a new place that has allowed me to be a source for other women who are going through changes in their lives and relationships. It was in that moment that I was being my natural self that I realized this is my gift—my calling. However, God had to disrupt my current situation to put me in that space for me to realize that this is my assignment. Had the ground not rumbled and the earthquake not shaken me up and separated me from all that I knew, I would not be in the position that I am today encouraging the many women that I am. For that I am forever grateful. I even look at the term "my divorce" differently. I now view it as something that had to occur for me to do greater in my life with my life, which to me is a blessing. Yes, there was devastation and initially a lack of understanding. When you do understand though, you consider things differently, you begin to look at life differently, and you view life differently. Instead of me looking at my life as a tragedy, I scrutinized everything that had occurred and found the opportunities for growth and whether a greater purpose existed in those circumstances. That is how we determine what the other side looks like. If you have a "Woe, it's always me" perception, you will continue to remain in the darkness because you weren't seeking the light. That's the one thing I never allowed myself to do was to create a pity party for myself, as there was nothing good in that mindset that could help me help myself.

Our seasons of darkness are also our seasons of opportunity and transformation. Be your own "shero." Who is in charge of you? Who are you going to blame your life on today? Even if they are participants in creating your current circumstances, you are still responsible for the end result of your life. No one else. That responsibility doesn't rest with a spouse, ex-spouse, family member, friend, or foe. That responsibility always remains on your shoulders because you are in control of your own destiny at all times. Be the "shero" of your own story.

Your life is a journey, which consists of hills, mountains, valleys, and even oceans where sometimes you just feel like you're drowning and trying to breathe for air. At the end of the day, the power is inside of you. What is your mindset? How are you positioning yourself for that breakthrough? What specifically are you creating to keep you focused and victorious rather than a victim of your circumstance? What does that look like? It all comes down to your time and how you are spending it. Are you spending your time dwelling on what no longer is? Are you spending your time dwelling on the past? Are you spending your time on something that has already happened and that nothing can be done about it? Those precious 24 hours of the day that we are given can't be taken back. Those 24 hours of the day need to become dynamic and need to be lived with intention— intention with you moving forward to something *greater*. How is this accomplished? First, change your mindset and know that you are making a commitment to do better, to be better, and to strive for greatness. What that equals to is being a "go-getter." It's time to put strategy in everything you do in this moment because every decision that you make has a consequence. This is the time for you to get your faith and finances in order, relationships that support you, and find what makes you feel centered and whole, which is essential. What makes you completely still and able to absorb like a sponge in a calm way peace in your life? It may be a good book or what I adore lighting candles, moving slowly, and not rushing or being consumed with so many things that nothing else can be processed. It's time to declutter, to declutter your mind, and to declutter your environment. I will speak about that in the following section titled, "The Power of Small Changes," As small changes can help you to achieve sustainability and happiness in a greater way.

When we are confused and unsure of ourselves, frequently we seek external validation, which is not needed. You only need your validation of who you are. Why do you feel the need to want to be accepted? Accept yourself and know that is what is consequential because no matter which person accepts you externally if you don't accept yourself internally, the acceptance that you're seeking won't hold the value that you think it does. You have to build yourself up from the inside out. You have to already be validated, which is self-validation, and consist of those valuable riches that we find in the darkness of who we are that take us to the next level. So, the next time you feel darkness in your life remember that it could very well be an opportunity presenting itself. Opportunities do not always have to come in the most conventional ways. Many times they come when you are at what you feel is a dark space. Steve Harvey mentioned at his "Act Like a Success Conference" how when seeds are planted, they have to push through the dirt in order to thrive and grow. This is no different. To get to the other side you have to continue to push through, although it will not always be easy, believe me. If I told you that it was going to be easy, I would not be serving you any truth because the struggle is real; however, it is also worth it. The struggle is a teaching moment of values and perseverance and represents all of the things that create a phenomenal character. We build our character based on how we react to our circumstances, and that character is who we become and what carries us to and through our various missions in life (many of us have several). So, again, embrace the darkness. Know that this is a moment that you can either "break" or "thank." You can thank God for this moment and ask what it is that I need to learn through the following prayer, "Lord, please bring me understanding and clarity so that I can serve for your purpose and not from my own understanding." It was in this moment of rediscovering who I was that I found it to be so refreshing to be able to be vulnerable to myself and to just allow life to happen. When you allow yourself to be susceptible and turn on your awareness, you pay attention to the things that you do, what things to do or not to do for you, and determine how best to respond. It's when we get knocked down that we find out what we are really made of. Be your own "shero."

The Power of Small Changes

Getting Organized

Often, we wonder why can't we just get it together? Why is that things just don't make sense to us? Why do we feel so overwhelmed? The answer to all of those questions is that we aren't organized. Organization isn't something that is only needed in our work environment, it is also something that we should practice in our homes. How organized are you at home? It's impossible to move forward without organization, since our day-to-day activities should be organized and we should be strategic in how we approach what it is that we are setting out to do. How do we accomplish this? I have a dream, I have a vision, and I have a goal that I'm setting— but how will I making them come to fruition without being organized? Organization is crucial in order for you to achieve the success that you desire. Without organization, the dreams and visions are something that sound good with no real action behind it. Measurable actions must be put into place so that you know whether something is working.

That's why you feel all over the place—because really you are! When I was transitioning to being a single mom, I had to sit and think about the following: What's next? What does my life look like now? and What do I want *it* to look like? Earlier, I referenced my wanting to help other women overcome their adversity, but that didn't come to me right away. I had to "declutter," a part of which involves eliminating all of those negative emotions, all of those negative chatterers in your head, and all of the people in your life who are not bringing you purpose. I had to get organized with an intent on understanding what it is that I wanted my next chapter to look like.

So, I sat down and I began to map it out. I knew that I've always loved to help others, and I looked at what it is that was a part of me that could remain so that I did not lose what I identified with. I created a Vision Wall, where I focused on an area with my kids and what I wanted to achieve with them. I knew that I wanted to continue to be a great parent, create a fund for them for college, continue

216

to go on vacations, serve my community, and write my book. This very book that you're reading right now was on my Vision Wall. I put intention on my wall, including that I will sit on Oprah's couch, that I will be on Steve Harvey's set, and that I will meet Iyanla Vanzant. In addition, included on my Vision Wall were words of inspiration from the infamous Dr. Maya Angelou that, "Nothing will work unless you do." That is one of the truest statements that could ever be said. In fact, I use this statement in my signature on my work e-mail and it serves as a reminder that it's not about how I'm feeling or what I don't feel like doing on some days. It serves as a reminder that if I'm in that right space that no matter what nothing is going to work unless I do the work—absolutely nothing. It was imperative for me to understand that and to comprehend that I had to let go of the negative chatter and the enemy of the people who were trying to bring me down in my life at that time.

Today, tomorrow, or 10 years from now, there's going to be rejection and people who will not serve your higher good. You must be willing to let go of all of the distractions because they will hinder your progress. You have to strike them down as soon as you recognize them because you know and understand that their presence will not be advantageous. Living with intent is getting organized and selective of who is in your circle. Does this person support me? Will this person knock me off my game because I'm spending energy that I shouldn't have to spend towards resistance? You have to become intentional about that. You have to protect your space. Good Lord, let me say it again! You have to protect your space. You have to be your own gatekeeper. That's living with intention. That's getting organized. Get organized with who is surrounding you because you will only be as good as the company that you keep.

My suggestion to you right now is to ask yourself the following questions:

What is it that I see in my head?

_____

_____

_____

_____

What is this vision I have that keeps resurfacing yet
I don't feel like I'm moving towards it?

_____

_____

_____

_____

_____

What actions have I taken?

_____

_____

_____

_____

_____

Who are my supporters?

_____

_____

_____

_____

_____

Who do I get good vibes from? Who's on my team?

_____

_____

_____

_____

Who is it that I need to get rid of? Who should I no longer give any of my energy?

_____

_____

_____

_____

_____

Then, you start planning what all of this is going to look like for you. *This is called decluttering.* This is both the mental and physical process, which at the beginning stages opens up so many more possibilities because you are able to receive, almost like your cell phone. You know how once your cell receives so much data the memory is full and you have to delete some apps and photos or transfer them over to make room for some space? It's no different for yourself. You can only hold so much internally and you want that content to be of value. If it isn't, trust me, you don't want it in your temple.

This brings me to my next point. *Declutter your environment.* As simple as this sounds, I promise you it's one of the greatest things that you can do. What does your environment look like? Are there clothes in the corner? On the floor? Is the kitchen unkempt? Your bedroom...What does your sanctuary look like? The place where you lay your head at night—Is it full of books stacked up on the nightstand or a dresser just full of junk that you say from time to time I have to get to or sort through that? Do you know that every time you look at something in your home that you're unpleased with that it's wearing on you because you aren't doing anything about it? It's time to do something about it if you're serious about getting organized. These small changes are so powerful because not only are they revisions that are changing you externally, these factors are helping to change your internal mindset. Don't take the small changes for granted when you wonder the following: Why can't I move forward? Why isn't this working for me? Why can't I focus? It's because you're not doing the work and the work doesn't start with what you're doing at your business, at work, or with the kids. Focus starts in your immediate surroundings and how you feel about your immediate surroundings is what you carry with you. What you receive and perceive is what you, in turn, deliver. So, when I say that, I mean it. What you receive as far as how you feel about what's going on around you, you're delivering that through frustration and a lack of clarity because of one simple thing that you can do, which is declutter. Make things make sense. When things make sense in your life, I promise it will be so much better for you, and you will wonder why you didn't do this a long time ago.

I had been focusing my energy on all of the wrong things. Be intentional about making your bed every single day so that when you come back into that sanctuary it's there to greet you and you feel good about looking at it. Make it a place that *you* want to go and that you desire to go at the end of the day. Create a separate workspace from your bedroom if you have a makeshift office in there. Make your bedroom a sanctuary just for the purpose of release. It doesn't take much—the small changes. In your organization make time for you. Embrace self-care, which you can have while you're in the process. I mention several times throughout the book that I love the glow, the ambiance, and the smell of candles, which create a mood of calmness. This sets the tone for the day and allows me to look at what I'm doing as a process of decluttering, as opposed to a chore. So, my question to you is: Are you ready for change by making the small changes that will bring clarity, fulfillment, and open up room for much-needed space in your life?

Be Everything to Yourself First

"Be Everything to Yourself First," is so much more important than people realize. The title itself is powerful. **Since the dissolution of my marriage was initiated,** I have learned and valued this more than ever, and I say that from a holistic approach. You must be everything to yourself first before you can be everything to someone else because you cannot pour from an empty cup. One of the things that I've done and I know that many women do, is become too vulnerable to a fault where our decisions aren't based on what's always in our best interest. Unfortunately, many of our decisions are based on emotion and how others make us feel or that we want to be loved and be in a relationship. I've made this mistake more than once, and this pattern started when I was a teenager. I've always dated older men or at that time older young men. I understand that this was partly because of my advanced maturity and practically raising myself, which placed me on a more advanced emotional level than most young women who were my age. I say that to say because as young women a lot of us come from families that don't necessarily express love in a way that we need it, to guide us, and to make better decisions. As we go out on our own, we have to fend for ourselves and through mistakes realize that the decisions that we are making are not necessarily the best decisions to be made. An example of this is when we see a guy or a guy sees us and he shows us a little attention. Right there, we're hooked. We're not necessarily hooked to that person because they are so great and they are just that good to us because we don't know that yet. We literally give ourselves away before we even know anything about this person and men prey on that, especially young women who show that they do not have the confidence in themselves. So it is important to be patient and really figure out who this person is. Take the time to figure that person out.

A way to avoid this is to be everything to yourself first. Your circumstances do not have to determine the decisions that you make in the future just because you were not loved at home or you did not receive affection that you witnessed other friends' families show. I can attest to that as well. When I was younger, I had many friends whose parents doted over them and their children were everything. So, I know how that feels, but that still doesn't give you a pass or an excuse to make decisions that will later cost you. When I was younger, a guy did not necessarily even have to be attractive to catch my attention. However, because he showed me a little bit of attention, that was all I felt that I needed. I felt that was love and the cycle continued relationship after relationship because later on it would be discovered that I knew this person was not the person for me. Had I taken the time to discover that instead of feeding off my emotions to want to be wanted, the end result could have been different for me. The need to want to be wanted is less when you are everything to yourself first because when you're everything to yourself first, you know exactly what your expectations are. You know exactly what you will and will not deal with. You know exactly how to approach or not to approach relationships.

Nearly 2 years later after my separation, I really value the value in being everything to myself first and it's not selfish. This doesn't necessarily have to be a romantic relationship. This can be a relationship with your children, a relationship with your family, or a relationship with your friends and/or coworkers. The more you are to yourself and fulfilling to yourself, the more you can be to everyone else. The more that you pour into making yourself happy and making yourself educated and finding out who you are, being in touch with your center, the better parent you can be or the better parent you will be for your children.

In addition, when you are your authentic and true self and happy with who you are, it shows and this becomes your legacy. You want your children to look back and to say great things about you. You want those memories to be wonderful memories of who their parent is. After many mistakes along the way in choosing my relationships, most times without the wisest reasons to do so and after realizing the pattern, I felt compelled to share my message, even now going through a divorce. I am not particular at this moment about having a relationship with anyone in the near future. I believe that in the process of being everything to yourself first, you have to be emotionally available in order to move forward. You must have things in place in your life that allow you to move forward. In addition to your emotions, which include your finances, stability, home life, and work life. I believe that one of the main reasons there is such a crisis in the percentage of failed marriages and relationships as a whole is because we are dealing in a society with broken people, and a large number of them. We don't give ourselves time to bounce back. Instead, we're bouncing forward on a rebound, and we don't give ourselves time to readjust, to assess, and to figure out who we are. We take our broken pieces and our broken hearts and we move on to the next person who more than likely is broken too because no one allows themselves to heal. Then, the cycle repeats itself. That convoluted process is where broken children come from because you now have broken people who have kids. Then, they are going through their various issues because they already had problems prior to entering into the new relationship. Now that relationship ceases. Now the children are broken.

Then, depending upon how that situation goes. If the parents aren't equally collaborating with one another and have a healthy, co-parenting relationship, the children see that and then they are broken in a different way. They are broken in the sense that they are learning that parents don't get along when there's a separation. This is what their mind is taking in since as you know children are human sponges. They take all of this in and then everybody's doing double work trying to "unbreak," which I know is not a word. Focus on fixing yourself first and being sure that you're ready to move forward instead of just getting someone to fill that void, which eventually gets old. Then, you move on to the next person because you feel something is wrong with that person who no longer fills their void, and that cycle continues. However, the person who really needs the work is you, and everyone is affected when these decisions are made. Be everything to yourself first before you decide to selfishly be what you call everything or available to someone else. We are a part of this problem, and until we do something about it, we will continue to be a broken society. As Toni Braxton says, "Unbreak My Heart." That takes time, patience, courage, respect for yourself, and respect and consideration for others.

Sometimes, you have to get knocked down lower than you have ever been to stand back up taller than you ever were!

THE PIVOTAL MOMENT: LIVING LIFE TO ITS FULLEST

Divorce is definitely a "tables turned up time" in anyone's life and a period where life-long dreams are shattered, visions are dimmed, and lives are sometimes changed forever until the next one comes along. For me, my life was changed in a way that I needed but did not know it was what I necessitated. Divorcing my husband was also an opportunity for me to divorce my old self and old thinking to become more of who I am today than I would have ever been had I remained married. Don't get me wrong, this does not put any bad feelings on my marriage. I've already said that I loved my husband, I loved our marriage, and all of the ups and downs associated with the relationship. I was "in it to win it." Unfortunately, a relationship takes two very willing individuals and that didn't happen. The result, however, was a blessing.

I had to divorce what I was used to, what I thought I had, and realize that everything happened for a reason. I had to acknowledge some things about myself that had those things not taken place I wouldn't have been able to see what I needed to really see about me. That's what divorce accomplishes. When you take the time out to fully process what it is that you're going through, you'll learn more about yourself and who you are. It is a necessary process that sometimes takes the separation between you and another person to show that you need some work. It may be that you were giving so much of yourself to others that you didn't really understand who you needed to be to you. Alternatively, it could be that you learned some things about yourself that you were uncomfortable with because you thought you had it all together when you really didn't. It's when you're faced to be with yourself by yourself without someone else that you only see a reflection of who you are only without the effort of taking care of others. Yes, most of us still have children that we have to look after. Admittedly, it's a lot different than having a man or a husband who requires attention as well, as those responsibilities are different in their own right. A pivotal moment in my life was my divorce, and it showed me that I needed to show up bigger now than ever because I never saw myself divorcing. This is something that I did not prepare for, which means that I needed to show up quick, and be willing, able, and ready to provide for my children as a single mother and as a broken woman, searching to heal my brokenness while helping others as a broken person inside. I was healing others and continued to heal others from a different broken spirit. It's the spirit of what broke me but what did not hold me broken in a negative space. Yes, that's a completely different type of "broken." This is a broken that I'm full of gratitude for because through the process I've learned more about who I am, my capabilities, what I can do for me, and what I can do for others, which is irreplaceable. This significant life event was a pivotal moment because for once in my life I challenged myself to be still, not be in a hurry to find the next Mr. Right, be present, and available to myself. That's a damn good feeling! Now, that's not to say that I won't ever enter into another relationship, but trust and believe that I'm not in any big hurry because I'm enjoying *me*! Celebrate yourself and the fact that now you have more time for you and with your children, which goes by very quickly, since before you know it, they'll be grown and out of the house. Men are already grown when you get them, and they're just a companion. You can't get those years back with your children and that's what I'm enjoying right now. I really don't feel the need to have a new man in my space to be a part of that. We love going on our road trips and being a part of each other. My children are even writing books now, the process in which I participate. So just when you look at divorce as being a life event that is often compared with "death," honey, let me tell you that divorce can be *your resurrection*. It's a chance for a new life.

You may hear that you only have one life to live and that life is short, but it's all on YOU and your perception. I may not have nine lives, but I did just start my second and I feel great about it. This was the pivotal part in my divorce—when my husband told me that he loved me but just didn't love me the same and felt that we had grown apart. In the following couple of days, I felt as if I was falling apart and that my life had ended. Looking back all I can say is, "Won't He do it?" Trust me when I tell you that I've been there and now that I'm finally on the other side, I see that it was truly never that bad. It's an illusion that we create because of our own reasons of embarrassment or the feeling that the person who we were supposed to be with forever will never be replaced—I really was dying inside; however, all of those feelings are temporary and *you will get through it!* Take it from someone who could never see herself without her husband in her life. I'll just leave it at that. You couldn't tell me that this was not the man who I wasn't going to grow old with, still rubbing his ashy feet and bad knees. You simply couldn't tell me that I was going to be with anyone else. We all change over the years, but that's a part of life. There are always going to be times when you don't like each other and things that are going to change that you may not be so particular about. But, these circumstances don't change your love or at least they shouldn't. That's a part of the whole relationship process— being able to grow through those changes and that's what we look forward to: the good, the bad, the happy, and the sad.

Unfortunately, not everyone will make it, we didn't. What I did create, though, is a Chapter Two. Have I given up on love? No way! I'm filled with love. What I have gained, though, is the wisdom in knowing that it's okay to take my time and to prepare myself for that next time. Right now, I'm full of gratitude at a time where most would feel pain, regret, and sorrow. That's when I know that I've overcome, I'll be alright, I'll be on the other side, and more fulfilled than I've been before because now I view life differently. I've had more experiences that have bettered me as a woman, as a mother, and potentially as a future wife.

Better days are ahead. Do know that. Be blessed.

DEDICATION TO MY UNCLE JOHNNY

I was conflicted about sharing this part of my journey. It wasn't until I woke up one night thinking about a situation when the memory of one of my favorite people in the world, my Uncle Johnny, resurfaced with something that he always said, "Be Cool. Be Cool." It was at that moment that I realized that what had been tugging at me for so long, wondering whether his story was a good fit for this book, that I realized it was indeed perfect because his story plays a significant part in who I am and my journey. This chapter also pays homage to one of the few people who have had an enormous impact on my life.

This is for you, Unc!

BE COOL... BE COOL...

Let's Go Roscoe

Due to the previously mentioned circumstances between my mother and myself that took place inside of our household, I spent the majority of my life with other relatives outside of my immediate family. In the midst of the tragedies that I've endured, I have also received many blessings, one of which is having one of the greatest uncles in the world be a part of my life and that was my uncle Johnny, who was also affectionately known as "Unc." Uncle Johnny and I were so close that he called me his Ace as he was also mine. We even share a birthday 1 day a part; mine is January the 3rd and his, January the 4th. He would always carry me around to different places. I have so many fond memories of us, including going fishing and visiting California to see his family. During one of these visits, he actually surprised me with a 5th birthday party on the plane! I can remember the flight attendant bringing me five delicious cupcakes. I blew out the candles and everyone on the plane sang "Happy Birthday" to me. This is one of my very special memories of our time together. I also remember how "Unc" gave me my very first birthday party at my nursery school. Unc was more than just an uncle; he was my dad. I owe my love of crabs to him. From the time I learned to eat crabs under the awning in his backyard with him and my Aunt Bert, who was actually my great Aunt by blood, and Uncle Johnny is her husband, all the way up to the time he left this earth, we both shared a love for crabs. It was a "no matter what thing" with us.

I remember during the time I had met my husband that Uncle Johnny was one of the first people who I told about him and mentioned how special he was to me. Then, I introduced them, which is something I never did—just take anyone around my Uncle—and it was then that I knew that I was going to be pretty serious about him. It was funny because initially Uncle Johnny was not very receptive to my husband, listening more so than talking. Of course, we were just dating at this time and he was not officially my husband. Uncle Johnny would just listen and nod a head here and there as if he was sizing him up and seeing what he was all about. Eventually, that relationship grew into a bond between my husband and Unc. In fact, in 2005 they both set me up on Thanksgiving, which was a few short months after our beautiful daughter Natalie was born. My husband and I resided in an apartment located in Windsor Mill, Maryland at the time and I recall being in the kitchen cooking and cleaning up for the day when the phone rang. It was Uncle Johnny. He said, "Hey, Shorty," which is something that he only called me. I was his "Shorty." He continued to say, "What are you doing tomorrow" and of course this was Thanksgiving Day. I told him that I didn't have any plans and that I was going to cook something at home. I also told him that was hoping that he would come up for the day because we usually spent our holidays together no matter what and no matter who I was with. It was a family tradition for me. Since I was born, my Thanksgivings, Christmases, and New Years were spent with my family, and through the years I did everything that I could for that not to change. For the most part, it didn't. Anyway, Unc continued to say, "Well, I want you and your hubby to come down. I want you to meet Mrs. Jones." This did not wave a red flag to me because there actually was a woman who I would tease my uncle about who he started dating after my aunt passed away and her name was Mrs. Jones. Therefore, I really thought that he finally wanted me to meet her.

What happened that next day was epic and the best prank ever! They really got me. We arrived at Uncle Johnny's house and per usual all three of us sat at the kitchen table, the same one that I used to sit at when I was a little girl. All of a sudden, my mother walks in, which was quite surprising to say the very least, as we already know how I feel about her. So, I kept it cordial. She joined us and I believe she put some pies in the oven. As time went by, I was still expecting Mrs. Jones to arrive and join us for the dinner. Then, my husband suggests that since it's Thanksgiving we should all participate in a roundtable and say a little something about what and why we're thankful, which started with my mother, followed by my Uncle Johnny, myself, and last my husband. Through teary eyes, he talked about what he was thankful for, saying how special I was to him and that he knew I was the person with whom he wanted to spend the rest of his life. He continued saying that the moment couldn't be more special and that what he was doing couldn't be done in a more special place because it was at the house of someone who I truly held close to my heart. So, I'm looking at him wondering what in the world is going on and that's when he said that he was thankful for me, bent down on one knee, and asked me to marry him. All I could think of at the moment was that this is crazy and the only words that could come out of my mouth were, "You're lying, you're lying, oh, my gosh, you're lying!" Then, that crazy uncle of mine said, "Would you say something instead of 'You're lying, you're lying'?" I finally said, "Yes." It was the funniest thing ever! I was pranked! It still didn't dawn on me until later when I said, "Well, when is Mrs. Jones going to get here?" My uncle looked at me and said, "You are Mrs. Jones." I thought about it and all I could say was, "Wow," because literally that is who I was going to be, Mrs. Jones, and that could not have worked out any more perfectly because his friend and I knew of her, I had never met her, but her name was indeed Mrs. Jones. He used the perfect plan to get me over there without being suspicious when in reality I was becoming Mrs. Jones. On the way home I guess through the roll of the night when we parked, guess what song came on? *Me and Mrs. Jones!* That's my funny little story.

Back to my uncle who shared all of these special moments with me. He was there for me and for my children, adoring them as much as he adored me. He was like their grandfather. He always wanted them around, to come see us, and that was how we rolled. Speaking of rolling, I recall that whenever we were on the road in my younger years, my Unc used to drive with the radar so that he could speed when "the boys" (police officers) were out on the road, checking for speeding. He was always just a cool guy and he was always sporty in his old Toyota Celica, where his license plate spelled out "Mai Toi." He and his best friend, Mr. Smitty, who recently passed, used to DJ together back in the day, and the name of their DJ gig was the 14th Flo Disco. I recall Uncle Johnny taking me on different gigs with him and just being his road dog. It was like yesterday that I can remember him saying, "Let's go, Rosco!" I find myself today using a lot of the same verbiage with my own children that he used with me. In many ways I pay homage to him naturally just through the bond that we had.

The Later Years

In 2010, Unc had suggested that we have a birthday together because that's something that we had never done. Earlier in this section, I mentioned that our birthdays were 1 day apart. I listened to him and knew from that moment immediately that I was going to plan a birthday party for him, as this was going to be his 85th birthday celebration. What he did not know is that I was going to make it all about him. I invited different family members, some of his neighbors, and his best friends, which included Miss Olivia, who lives in Colorado, as well as Mr. Smitty and others. I let everyone know that we were going to come together for Unc's birthday. In the year 2011, Unc had moved in with my family because he wanted to be closer to us since he would frequently drive up from near Washington, DC all the way to our home, which is located more than 60 miles away near Delaware on the Maryland side. I remember this year so vividly, as it was the beginning of "The War," which I will discuss later.

During this time my uncle had made several changes and things started to evolve with the relationship between me, Unc, and his daughter, who I had actually just learned about after my aunt had passed away. When Unc and my aunt separated for a couple of years, he had a love child and when they reconciled I learned through my uncle that the agreement between them was that my uncle would not have anything to do with this child. I disagree with my aunt for this stance because if she loved him enough to take him back, that child was now a part of him and she needed to accept the whole package because that child had nothing to do with his decisions. Although I was shocked, I was very excited to meet my uncle's daughter, who was old enough to be my mother, and her children. In 2011, things really began to change in their relationship, so much so that he called me up one day and said, "Shorty, get down here quick, right now!" and he changed everything, including his banking information, he wrote his daughter out of his will, and removed her from being his Power of Attorney. I mean it was crazy to me. I didn't know exactly what took place until he told me that he was tired of being mistreated by her and that he knew that she was just waiting for him to pass so the she could inherit his wealth. Of course, this was heartbreaking to me and I've always been one to help my senior family members avoid any maltreatment or to prevent someone from taking advantage of them.

247

To my surprise while we were driving to my home because my uncle did not want to stay in his house once she realized the changes that he had made, he says, "Well, what am I going to do with all of this money"? The money that he had me go to his bank and cash out was significant and in the six figures. He decided that he wanted to leave it to me and said, "Pay the Government folks off." He was speaking about my student loans. I was so overwhelmed and could not stop thanking him for blessing me in such a way.

Unc was both a big part of my family and my existence. With all that I've experienced I could have been led down the wrong path. It's not that I was perfect, as I've made mistakes, but my life would not be what it is today if it was not for the Uncle Johnnys, Elaines, and Berts in my life. So this is why I had to do this chapter.

Then, it was April 21st, 2012, when my world once again shattered. Unc had transitioned into his new life in heaven. I have no words for the empty feeling that was in my heart at the time. I literally felt as if I lost my best friend. Although I knew he was with me in spirit, it would not be the same for me here on earth, even eating crabs would not be the same for a very long time. It was not only a sad time for me, it was the beginning of a very dark period. It was the beginning of a war.

During such a time of significant loss for me, is when as expected, Uncle Johnny's daughter showed up and showed out, coming after everything he had. This has now turned into a 4-year court battle. When I tell you that "The Battle is Not Yours," it is not! It's the Lord's. This woman has tried every trick in the book to wrongfully denunciate me and God stepped in and made sure that the right person won the match. She and her attorney stooped as low as involving my husband as a witness on their behalf! You read right! This man turned on me once again, in my Uncle's estate case. Once again he was in the chair testifying against his wife. He was also disappointing the man that he at one time endearingly loved and called, "Pop." If only Unc could speak from the grave.....Ah, but he did! Victory is ours! I remember during the trials, I wrote on a sticky note, "Be cool…be cool" to feel his presence in the room.

I miss that guy dearly, but know that he is up above watching over me and making sure that I remain cool…. ☺

My final message to you as you close this book, is
to whether the storms with great intention of
learning the lesson to be learned, while having the
faith and courage to push through to the other side.
In the process,
Don't sweat the small stuff, just…

Be COOL!

NOTES

_____

_____

_____

_____

_____

_____

_____

_____

_____

_____

_____

_____

_____

_____

_____

_____

_____

_____

_____

_____

_____

NOTES

NOTES

NOTES

* 9 7 8 0 6 9 2 8 2 9 1 9 6 *